Padua

Pier Luigi Fantelli

Padua

Electa

Introduction
The first part of the guide gives a brief historical outline of the development of the city of Padua.

The Visit
The second part of the guide consists of a series of suggested itineraries for visiting the city. This section begins with a *city map* which shows the churches, palaces and other places of interest which are described in detail in the text.
The names of the *buildings and monuments* of historical and artistic significance described in the text are printed in bold type.
The titles of *works of art* are printed in italics in the text.
Each itinerary is described with an introductory text which draws the reader's attention to the most important buildings. The *buildings and monuments* of historical and artistic significance, which can be easily found on the map by means of the references given, are then listed in order in the section dedicated to the area where they are located; for each of these *buildings and monuments* there is a description of the history, details regarding the works of art, any rebuilding or restoration work that may have been carried out and their present condition.

Cover
Giorgio Fossati, *A Horse Race in the Prato della Valle*, 1767. Padua, Museo Civico.

Translation
David Stanton

Contents

A Historical Outline and the Growth of the City

According to the historians of antiquity it was Antenor, the Homerian hero and advocate of peace between the Greeks and Trojans, who founded the city of Padua when he reached the upper Adriatic in his flight from the Achaeans. This legend, which was referred to by Virgil in the *Aeneid*, has no historical foundation: in fact, archaeologists have established that, although the area has been inhabited since the 12th century B.C., it was only in the 8th century B.C. that a settlement was founded in the heart of what is now the present city on an island formed by the splitting of the River Brenta into two loops. Known in Latin as the Medoacus, the city's development was to be concentrated along its banks. As proof of the important role it played, Livy refers to a temple dedicated to Juno in the centre of the city where the booty was displayed when it was taken from Cleomenes, the Spartan king who was defeated by the Paduans in 302 B.C. when he attempted to conquer the city. The legend is testimony to the existence of sacred sites linked to water as early as the 4th century B.C., and it was the river that governed the development of pre-Roman Padua, with the necropolises situated to the north on its former eastern course (Via S. Massimo, Via G.B. Belzoni, Via G.B. Tiepolo), also within the two loops in the Medoacus. The outward growth of the city from this early core reflected this plan even after Padua had been gradually drawn into the Roman sphere of influence, from the time of the wars against the Cisalpine Gauls in 226 B.C. up to the inclusion of Patavium in the *X Regio* and the introduction of Roman law in 49 B.C. The river was the main route for commerce and on it was situated the port, the business centre of a city whose wealth was based on agriculture and trade, especially that of wool: the censuses of the Augustan period indicated as many as five hundred knights whose property was estimated as being worth 400,000 sesterces and in Strabo's day Padua was considered to be one of the wealthiest cities of the empire. Livy's *flumen oppidi medium* ("the river in the middle of the city"), on which the port stood near the forum, the central feature of the Roman city crossed by the imposing bridges — now buried — of San Lorenzo and Altinate. They linked the *insula* (island) formed by the loop in the Brenta which was laid out on the two axes formed by the *cardo* (north-south) and the *decumanus* (east-west), with the area which had developed towards the east on the road leading to Altino, the modern Via Altinate.

Outside the *pomerium*, the urban area, were located the theatre (the Zairo) in the present-day Prato della Valle and the amphitheatre, where the Arena Chapel now stands. Thus the city was one of the largest in the empire, where important routes met, the birthplace of Livy and Trasea Peto, who was famous for the *patavina severitas* ("Paduan severity"). Because of its close links with Rome it shared its decline from the 4th century onwards and was sacked by the Attila's Huns in 452-53. Meanwhile, in the mid-3rd century A.D. the first Christian church was built by Bishop Prosdocimus, whose cult flourished in the 5th and 6th centuries, when the city came into the Byzantine orbit (from 540 onwards): the orien-

Opposite

Giotto, Enrico Scrovegni Offering a Model of the Chapel Borne by the Prior of the Order of the Knights of Our Lady, to the Virgin, detail from the Last Judgement. Arena Chapel.

Limestone funerary stele, from Camin, near Padua, late 6th century B.C. Musei Civici agli Eremitani.

Limestone funerary stele with a battle between a knight and a naked foot soldier. From the necropolis in Via Leonardo Loredan, 3rd century B.C. Musei Civici agli Eremitani.

tal titles of some churches (Santa Sofia and Sant'Eufemia for instance) date from this period, as does the presence in Padua of the legendary King Vitalianus, the father of Saint Justina of Padua, the martyr to whom the basilica outside the walls founded by the praetor Opilione in the area of the Prato della Valle was dedicated. After it had been razed to the ground by the Lombards under Agilulf in 602, Patavium had to await the Frankish domination of the 8th century before it was able to benefit from urban renewal, favoured by the presence through the "dark ages" of a diocese: the first reference to a cathedral was made on the occasion of the burial of Bishop Tricidius at the beginning of the 9th century. Indeed, it may be safely assumed that the bishop's palace was at the hub of the first rebuilding of the city, which was aided by the privileges granted to the Paduan bishops in the mid-9th century. This development was, however, interrupted by the forays of the Hungarians at the beginning of the 10th century which compelled the Paduan bishops, with imperial authorization, to fortify their properties, including those situated in the city. Thus it was that the city regained the central role that had been taken over, after the destruction by the Huns, by the *comitatus* of Monselice: in 969 A.D. Padua became a *comitatus*, at the centre of a vast area. Although civil power began to grow in importance, that of the bishops remained strong; indeed, in 1079, with the concession by the Emperor Henry IV of the tithe property in the city, it became the driving force for development over the next two centuries, in which there was a notable expansion of the ecclesiastical structure, so that by 1178 there were already sixteen parishes. A fire four years previously had destroyed 2,614 buildings, while the earthquake of 1117 must have damaged also the more solidly constructed edifices. However, the urban development also had important effects on the city's political structure: at the end of the 11th century the Commune of Padua was functioning and this favoured trade by setting up the markets near the municipal building; it also began the construction of the first city walls along the river in 1195.

These served to enclose an urban area in which the population was growing rapidly and the economy and cultural activities were flourishing: signs of this were, on the one hand, the foundation of the university in 1222, which was an offshoot of the one in Bologna and, on the other hand, the establishment of monasteries around the city by the Benedictines, the Dominicans, the Augustinian Hermits and, above all, the Franciscans. In 1232, in the southern part of the city, the latter founded the basilica of Sant'Antonio, which was to become an outstanding feature of the urban scene on its site next to the Prato della Valle, the area where fairs were held. In this period the central markets were also given a permanent home with the building of the Palazzo della Ragione, which was not only the seat of the law courts and the municipal offices but also a large covered market: at the same time the construction of the city walls was under way and they were extended to include the new suburbs as they grew up. The capture of Padua by the imperial vicar Ezzelino da Romano (signore

1237-56) resulted in the continuation of the defensive works which culminated in the building of the castle in 1242. After the fall of Ezzelino, the Commune of Padua resumed its central role, while the new form of power, the signory, continued to assert itself. The layout of the city started to take on a more permanent form and, when the Carrara family began to rule—Giacomo I became capitano in 1318—it was they who surrounded Padua by the first complete wall in 1337. In this period the artists working in the city after Giotto and Giovanni Pisano included Guariento di Arpo, Giusto de' Menabuoi, Altichiero and Avanzo, while Petrarch was a guest of Francesco il Vecchio, and it was here that conditions were ideal for the formation of the pre-humanistic cultural milieu which gave rise to the Renaissance. The Carrara signory, which was responsible for the complete reconstruction of its palace and other architectural and town planning works, lasted until 1405, when the long period of Venetian domination began; it was only with the arrival of Napoleon at the end of the 18th century that this came to an end. On 30 January 1406 a golden bull decreed that Padua was to become part of the Venetian Republic; by and large Venice accepted the existing socio-political situation in the city, and this was specified in the statutes of 1420, which were revised in 1430. In fact, in the 15th century there was a period of economic recovery which favoured urban growth, especially as regards the construction of buildings that were more monumental in character, which, nevertheless, conformed to the pre-existent layout of the city and conserved the arcades lining the streets (as in Bologna); moreover, it paved the way for new developments in the arts, especially those of Tuscan origin.

From the first half of the 15th century Tuscan artists had been working in Padua, in particular after 1434 when Palla Strozzi took refuge in the city during his exile from Florence.

Pietro Chevalier, Antenor's Tomb, engraving, 1858.

Seal of the City of Padua, engraving in B. Scardeone, De antiquitate urbis Patavii, 1560. Biblioteca dei Musei Civici.

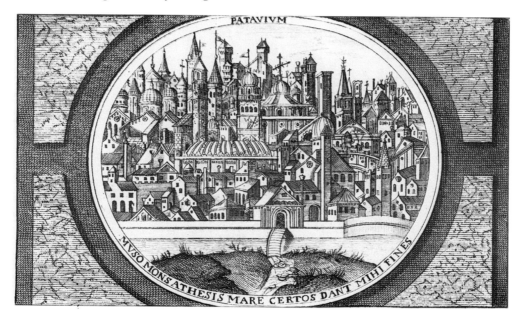

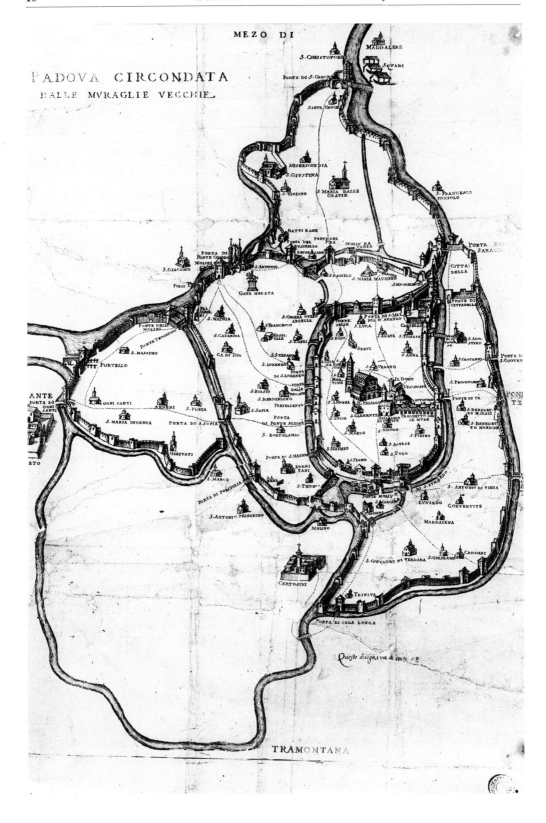

Thus, Paolo Uccello, Filippo Lippi and Donatello arrived in his train; at the same time Pietro Lombardo initiated the Renaissance style in architecture, which had hitherto been characterized by Venetian Gothic. The Tuscan influence was of fundamental importance for the formation of the Paduan school, including Nicolò Pizolo and Mantegna, while Donatello's workshop gave birth to the school of Paduan bronze-workers (Bartolomeo Bellano and Andrea Briosco).

The classicistic character, with its "archaeological" overtones, of the Paduan Renaissance continued during the 16th century, when the city, while maintaining its 14th century layout, underwent an architectural renewal: firstly Lorenzo da Bologna (San Giovanni da Verdara, the Palazzo Vescovile), then Falconetto (the Cornaro Loggia and Odeum) and Andrea Moroni (the university, the Palazzo Comunale) made a great contribution in this culturally vital period in which new developments in painting were heavily influenced by Titian's presence in the city in 1510-11: he was the source of inspiration for the Paduan school, including Gualtieri, Stefano dell'Arzere and D. Campagnola, which was perhaps the last truly coherent group of artists working in the city.

The crisis resulting from the formation of the League of Cambrai at the beginning of the 16th century, which threatened the very existence of the Venetian Republic, had in the meanwhile set in motion the process which gave Padua its present urban layout: in fact, by 1544 Fra' Giocondo, Michele Sanmicheli and Giovanni Maria Falconetto had built the fortifications which remained unaltered until the 19th century. In the city, in a socio-political context which was increasingly under the control of the Venetian nobility who invested in property there, the urban layout did not change, although space was left for new developments, the most striking of which was the formation of the Ghetto in 1601. However, the most important town planning scheme carried out under Venetian rule was the creation by Domenico Cerato, who received the commission from the podestà Andrea Memmo, of the Prato della Valle. It is worth noting that this is a meadow without grass, which is perhaps only right and proper in a city which has a saint without a name (Saint Anthony of Padua is known there simply as "the Saint") and a café without doors (the Caffè Pedrocchi, once open night and day).

The fall of the Venetian Republic, Austrian rule, then the kingdom of Italy had little effect on the overall plan of the city: however, during the 19th century a gradual transformation took place in the name of public health and progress, culminating in the demolition of part of the walls and, above all, the filling in of the canals, as well as the razing to the ground of some of the medieval quarters. This process continued until the 20th century to the north (the railway station) and along the main roads (westwards, especially in the direction of Milan), while the complete filling in of the inner canal, the ancient Medoacus on which the Roman river port was sited, was the last important measure taken to modernize the city, which today is grappling with problems that are similar to those faced by other Italian cities in their historic centres.

Opposite
Padua Surrounded by the Old Walls, engraving in A. Portenari, Della felicità di Padova, *Padua 1623.*

On the following pages
Map of the centre of Padua.

D. Danieletti, Plan of the Prato della Valle, engraving. Biblioteca dei Musei Civici.

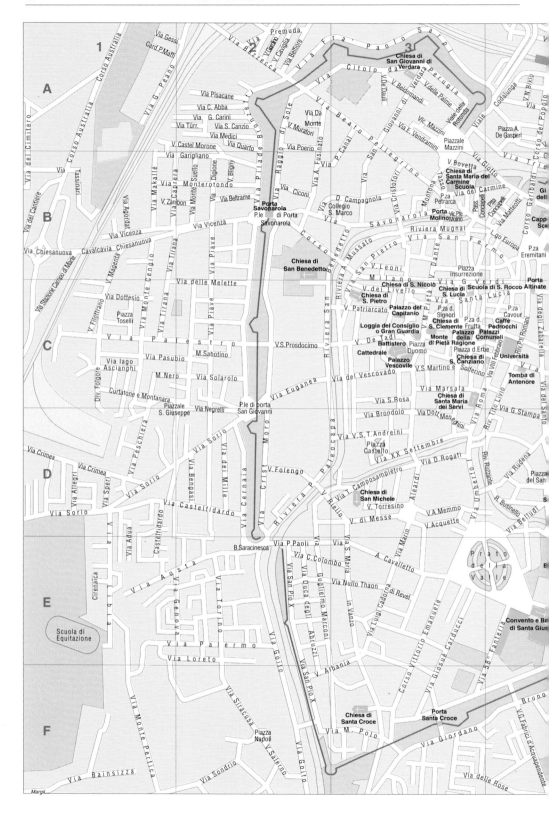

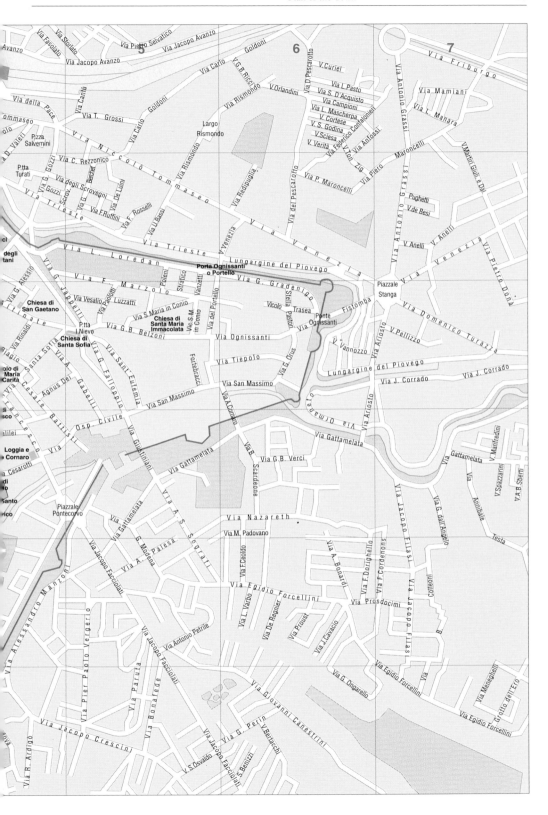

The Historic Centre

This is the civic, political and commercial heart of the old city, where it seems that the Roman forum was sited and where the markets were held; during the 13th century these were housed in the **Palazzo della Ragione**, popularly known as **Il Salone** due to its immense size.

To the east of this complex is situated that of the **Palazzi Comunali** (municipal buildings) which includes the **Palazzo degli Anziani** in Via Oberdan, which is the oldest of these buildings (1285) and has a long arcade that is separated by the **Torre degli Anziani** (1296) from the **Palazzo del Consiglio** built in 1283: here in the loggia at ground-floor level, now walled up, Byzantine capitals were used.

Behind these buildings is the **Palazzo del Podestà**, the present-day town hall, which was also built at the end of the 13th century, but was totally rebuilt on the basis of a project by Andrea Moroni in 1539-58. On the side facing the Piazza delle Erbe the palace rises from a rusticated arcade, while on the east side two covered staircases lead up to the hanging Doric courtyard, in the centre of which stands a well-curb.

To the north of the Piazza della Frutta lay the medieval quarter of Santa Lucia, which was almost entirely demolished in the 1920s to make way for the present Piazza Insurrezione, with only a handful of historic buildings being saved, including the so-called **Casa di Ezzelino**, which was built in the second half of the 12th century. Proceeding along the narrow Via Pietro d'Abano, which ends with a distinctive archway, the visitor comes to a small piazza with, on the right, the church of **Santa Lucia** and, at the far end, the **Scuola di San Rocco**, which was built in 1480 and extended in 1525.

To the south of the Piazza delle Erbe stretches the labyrinth of narrow streets forming the **Ghetto**, which was built at the beginning of the 17th century; in it there is the last **synagogue** of the three that once existed in the city. On the west side of the piazza stands the massive eclectic structure of the **Palazzo delle Debite**, built on the site of the old debtors' prison, in the vicinity of which was situated the small church of **Santi Canziano, Canzio, Canzianilla e Proto**. Via Fiume leads to the Piazza dei Signori, the centre of the power of the Venetian rulers, who sited the lion of Saint Mark here.

The façade of the church of **San Clemente**, where the most important *fraglie* (guilds) of tradesmen (apothecaries, butchers, blacksmiths, goldsmiths, farriers) once had their altars, stands on the eastern side of the piazza; to the south, on the corner of Via del Monte di Pietà, the **Loggia del Consiglio** or **Gran Guardia** may be admired. On the west side of the Piazza dei Signori there is the façade of the **Palazzo del Capitanio** built in 1599-1605 as the residence of the capitano, one of the two *rettori* (government representatives) in the city, as a replacement for the old palace of the Carrara.

The palace complex, which covered a large area of the medieval city, included the church of **San Nicolò**. From the Piazza Capitaniato, through the passageway of the **Scala dei Giganti** another courtyard of the old palace is reached; this is separated from the Piazza Duomo by the **Arco Vallaresso**.

The long arcade lining the north side of the piazza is part of

Opposite

A man on a dromedary and a woman collecting herbs, details of the month of April. Palazzo della Ragione.

the **Monte di Pietà**; this was built on the site of the old palace of the Scrovegni family that was destroyed by a fire and was known as the casa brusada ("burnt house").

PALAZZO DELLA RAGIONE (IL SALONE) (C3). One of the largest medieval buildings existing in Europe, it was built around 1218-19 as part of a scheme to reorganize the area of the central squares to accommodate the market stalls on the ground floor, offices and shops on the mezzanine floor and, on the upper floor, the law courts divided between the three large halls covered by a timber-trussed roof, supported by four wooden columns covered with leather. These were reached by four outside staircases which were named—according to the type of market held at their feet—*dei ferri* (tools), *del vino* (wine), *delle erbe* (herbs) and *degli uccelli* (birds). The need for more space led in 1306-1309 to the reconstruction of the building by Fra' Giovanni degli Eremitani, who was responsible for the roof having the form of an upturned boat, which was covered externally with lead sheets and supported internally by eleven ribs and iron tie-rods; this ceiling was decorated with a star-spangled sky, while the walls were painted with a fresco cycle inspired by Pietro d'Abano and Giotto and his workshop (1315-17), in which the medieval conception of astrology and cosmology were linked to the building's judicial function.

On 2 February 1420 a fire destroyed this structure, which was immediately rebuilt; after the upturned boat construction had been completed, along the sides were added two-tiered arcades incorporating the outside staircases, the doors of which were decorated with alto-relievos depicting Paduan personages (*Pietro d'Abano*, *Livy*, *Alberto Eremitano* and

Piazza delle Erbe, view of the Palazzo degli Anziani and the Palazzo del Consiglio with the Torre degli Anziani and part of the Vòlto della Corda.

Palazzo della Ragione, interior view with the wooden horse.

Giulio Paolo), while inside the astrological cycle was repainted by Nicolò Miretto and a Ferrarese assistant, so that the palace acquired its present appearance.

The upper floor is reached by the main staircase in the internal courtyard of the town hall, through the archway of the **Vòlto della Corda**. The walls are decorated with two rows of frescoes separated by the small arches of the string-course which indicates the height of the Salone before the present roof was built. The first register contains representations of real and imaginary animals, each of which corresponded to the seat of the court which was situated here.

In the middle register are the allegorical representations of *Virtues* by Giusto de' Menabuoi, the *Patron Saints* of Padua (on the four doors of the loggias), *Saint Mark* and the *Coronation of the Virgin* (on the west and east walls, 15th and 16th centuries), *Sacred Scenes* (on the site of the old church) and the *Coats of Arms* of the podestà of the city. The upper register, divided into 333 scenes arranged in three rows divided by fictive octagonal pillars, represents a vast celestial calendar in which astronomical figures appear together with the influences on men deriving from them on the basis of the astrological theories suggested by Pietro d'Abano.

Each month begins with an *Apostle,* according to the medie-

The pietra del vituperio; *following the exhortation of Saint Anthony this seat in black stone was installed in 1231 to punish insolvent debtors. The communal statutes of 1261 stated that the debtor, having removed all his clothes except his underpants and shirt (hence the Italian expression "to be left in one's underpants", meaning to be penniless), in the presence of at least a hundred worthy citizens, had to strike the stone thrice with his buttocks uttering the words "cedo bonis" ("I renounce my property"). After this he was expelled from the city.*

View of the "Casa di Ezzelino" with archway, from Via Marsilio da Padova. Although the legend that the building was the residence of the tyrant is unfounded, it certainly dates from the 13th century.

val tradition in which the signs of the zodiac corresponded to the twelve Apostles; this is followed by a *Sign of the Zodiac* and the representation of the *Planet* associated with the month. The cycle begins with the vernal equinox, followed by March on the south wall and continues on the west, north and east walls, in that order: the month of August has been substituted by September.

The whirlwind which destroyed part of the roof in 1756 also damaged the frescoes, which were repainted in 1770 by Francesco Zannoni.

The large **wooden horse** was made for a tournament organized in 1466 by the Capodilista family, and is a partial copy of Donatello's Gattamelata horse. On the west wall there are monuments to Livy (1547), with bronze sculptures by Agostino Zotto and frescoes by Domenico Campagnola, to Lucrezia Dondi Orologio (1661) by Tommaso and Matteo Allio and to Sperone Speroni by Marc'Antonio Sordi (1588-94). Rinaldo Rinaldi executed the bas-relief on the door of the Vòlto della Corda; this is dedicated to the Paduan explorer Giovan Battista Belzoni who presented two Egyptian statues to the city which were formerly in the Salone and are now in the Museo Civico. Next to it is the **pietra del vituperio**.

PALAZZI COMUNALI (C3). The complex of the Palazzi Comunali, situated between the university and the Palazzo della Ragione, includes the **Palazzo degli Anziani**, the **Palazzo del Consiglio** and the **Palazzo del Podestà**.

From the present inner courtyard two covered staircases lead up to the hanging Doric courtyard; in the centre of this stands a well-curb on which there are medallions and plaques commemorating figures who have played an important role in the city's history.

In the **Sala dei Matrimoni**, formerly the chapel of the Collegio dei Notai, is displayed the altarpiece by Domenico Campagnola depicting the *Virgin with Saints Anthony and Andrew* and there are frescoes representing *Scenes from the Lives of John the Baptist and John the Evangelist* by Pietro Damini da Castelfranco (restored and repainted by G. Cherubini in 1921). Damini also executed the large painting in the **Sala della Giunta** depicting the *Exchange of the Insignia of Power between the Two Podestà Valier*.

Remains of the late 16th century decoration of the rooms in the Palazzi Comunali are kept in the present **Sala dei Capigruppo**, where Lodewyck Toeput, called Pozzoserrato, painted frescoes with views of Padua and Venice.

CHIESA DI SANTA LUCIA (C3). Reference was made to this church in documents as early as 964, but it was only in 1308 that it became a parish church.

Aisleless from its origins, the church was rebuilt on the basis of a project by Girolamo Frigimelica under the direction of Sante Benato; the work, which started in 1711, was completed in 1728.

The design was based on the Palladian church of the Redentore in Venice, with an aisleless nave, presbytery and vault

comprising lunettes. The niches surrounding the nave con-
tain statues by Giovanni and Antonio Bonazza and their
workshop, while the paintings in the panels under the cornice
are by (above) Giovan Battista Tiepolo and Giacomo Ceruti,
called il Pitocchetto (c.1740).
In the first arch to the left of the entrance hangs the *Incredu-
lity of Saint Thomas*, the first dated work (1610) by Alessandro Varotari, called Padovanino.

Piazza della Frutta, view of the Palazzo della Ragione and the Palazzo del Podestà (from the beginning of Via Manin).

SCUOLA DI SAN ROCCO (C3). The *fraglia* (guild) of San
Rocco and Santa Lucia originally had its altar in the church of
Santa Lucia.
In 1468, thanks to a gift, it was possible to build the chapterhouse of the school next to this church and it was already
in use in 1480. In 1525 the *fraglia* bought a ruined house near
the church so that it could build a new chapterhouse there,
since the first one was too small: this building had been built
up to the roof in 1545, but as early as 1533 it was being decorated by Gualtiero Padovano and his assistants.
The interior of the building, which is on two floors, was originally decorated with frescoes throughout. While the frescoes
on the upper floor, the execution of which lasted from 1533 to
1559, no longer exist, on the ground floor the *Scenes from the
Life of Saint Roch*, one of the most interesting Cinquecento
fresco cycles in Padua, may still be admired.
Although payment was made from 1536 to 1545 to the painter
Gualtiero Padovano, he was assisted by Domenico Campa-

Church of Santa Lucia, façade.

Gualtiero Padovano, the Funeral of Saint Roch, detail. Scuola di San Rocco, left of the high altar.

Ghetto, view of Via dell'Arco. There has been a Jewish community in Padua since 1200, but only in the mid-16th century was a special area reserved for it; this was created in 1603 by shutting off an area to the south of the central squares with four gates.

gnola (*The Prayer of Saint Roch's Parents*), who was also responsible for the frieze in the presbytery, G. del Santo (Saint Rocco's birth) and Stefano dell'Arzere (*Lamentation for the Death of Saint Roch*), also attributed to Stefano Calcar. The painting on the high altar depicting the *Virgin and Saints* was executed by the Vicentine artist Alessandro Maganza.

SYNAGOGUE (C3). Of the three synagogues which formerly existed in Padua only the one in Via San Martino e Solferino, 9, which adheres to the Italian rite, has survived. It was built by Johannan Treves, Aron Salom and Moisè de Roman in 1548 and alterations were made in the 17th and 19th centuries; it was closed in 1892 and reopened after the Second World War.

The synagogue is entered by a staircase which leads to an external landing from which the women's gallery overlooking the staircase is also reached: the walls are covered with wood and lined with benches and there is a coffered ceiling.

The hall is divided into two parts by the *tevah* (pulpit) and the *aron* (torah ark); the latter is Baroque with black marble Corinthian columns and is placed between two carved chairs and six Corinthian columns with a baldachin (similar to the high altar of San Benedetto).

CHURCH OF SANTI CANZIANO, CANZIO, CANZIA-NILLA E PROTO (C3). It was known to exist since the 11th century, when it belonged to the monastery of S. Stefano. Used in the 13th and 14th centuries for the graduation of the art students, it was rebuilt at the end of the 16th century: this work had been completed by 1617.

The nave is flanked by two aisles: in the south one, on the altar, there is a terracotta statue representing the *Dead Christ* by Andrea Briosco, called il Riccio (c.1530); on the high altar, between terracotta statues of saints by Briosco there is an altarpiece depicting the *Virgin and Saints* by Alessandro Varotari, called Padovanino. Above the sacristy door there is the *Miracle of the Miser* by Pietro Damini in which, according to tradition, the surgeon who removes the miser's heart is a portrayal of the anatomist G.F. d'Acquapendente.

The Loggia della Gran Guardia.

LOGGIA DEL CONSIGLIO or GRAN GUARDIA (C3). After the fire in the Palazzo della Ragione in 1420, the Maggior Consiglio of Padua was moved to a building located in the area of the present loggia, which soon proved to be inadequate. In 1496 a competition for the design of the new building was held; although this was won by Annibale Maggi da Bassano his project was only realized from 1501 onwards, under the direction of Biagio Bigoio da Ferrara; in 1530 he was replaced by Giovan Maria Falconetto, who completed the work in 1545. On the upper floor, which has a wooden ceiling by Giovanni Paolo da Venezia, there is a fresco cycle representing Scenes from the *History of Padua* painted by the Bolognese artist P.A. Torri (1667-68) on the basis of the iconographic scheme drawn up by C. Dottori; this was inspired by the exemplary role played by the virtues of the forefathers.

Piazza dei Signori, view of the Palazzo del Capitanio with the Torre dell'Orologio.

Opposite

Domenico Campagnola, Vespasian, Curius Dentatus and Marcus Furius Camillus. Faculty of Arts (former Carrara palace), Liviano, Sala dei Giganti.

Sala dei Giganti, interior with frescoes. Faculty of Arts (former Carrara palace), Liviano. The present decoration of the Sala dei Giganti consists of forty-four colossal figures of Emperors (Giants) in fictive architectural structures, under which there are scenes and epigraphs regarding their lives. These frescoes were painted in 1540 by Domenico Campagnola, Stefano dell'Arzere and Gualtiero Padovano over a pre-existent cycle of famous men painted before 1379 by Guariento di Arpo, Altichiero, Jacopo Avanzo and Ottaviano Prandino following the directions of Petrarch: the portraits of Petrarch and his secretary Lombardo della Seta in their respective studies have remained on the west wall.

PALAZZO DEL CAPITANIO (C3). This is the former palace of the Carrara which was rebuilt in Venetian style, probably from the mid-16th century until the beginning of the 17th century: in Piazza dei Signori the **Torre dell'Orologio**, designed by Giovan Maria Falconetto was erected in 1532 together with the main entrance, while in the inner courtyard the **Loggia del Capitanio**, attributed to Andrea Moroni, was built (now the Faculty of Education). Vincenzo Dotto designed the main covered staircase (**Scala dei Giganti**) which links the two main halls in the complex in 1607; in the same year frescoes were painted by Gasparo Giona in the former Sala delle Udienze, now the **Sala delle Edicole**, on the east side; to the west the **Sala dei Giganti** was created by rebuilding the 14th century Sala degli Eroi of the Carrara palace.

The only remaining building of the Carrara palace is the two-tiered loggia on roseate marble columns (attributed to Domenico da Firenze, c.1343) which is now the seat of the Accademia Patavina di Scienze, Lettere ed Arti.

Here in the ground-floor rooms there are traces of decorations and fictive tapestries bearing coats of arms of the Carrara, while in the room for academic meetings on the upper floor, formerly the **Cappella Carrarese**, there are some fragments of the *Stories from the Old Testament* painted by Guariento in the mid-14th century. Guariento also decorated the ceiling with panels depicting the *Virgin*, *Angels and Saints*, some of which are now in the Museo Civico.

In 1937-39, on the site of the old palace, Gio Ponti designed and built the **Liviano**, the seat of the Faculty of Arts. A competition for the decoration was held in 1938 in which Mario Sironi, Ubaldo Oppi, Guido Cadorin and Massimo Campigli (sketches in the head of the faculty's office) took part: having won, in 1939-40 Campigli executed the frescoes, which re-

Church of San Nicolò, façade.

volve around the theme of the *Continuity of the Classical Culture in the Modern World*. In the entrance-hall is the marble *statue of Livy* after whom the faculty is named; Arturo Martini was commissioned to sculpt it in 1942 by the donor, Mario Bellini.

From the vestibule of the head of the faculty's office the **Museo di Scienze Archeologiche e d'Arte** is reached. This was also designed by Gio Ponti in 1937-39, who laid it out in three rooms which were intended to hold the nucleus of the historical collection; there is also an educational section and a gallery of plaster casts.

CHIESA DI SAN NICOLÒ (C3). This church was first mentioned in 1088 as being subject to the *ius patronatus* (right of patronage) of the Paduan monastery of San Pietro.

When, at the end of the 13th century, the old building was found to be inadequate it was rebuilt, but it was only in the 15th century that it assumed the present plan with a nave flanked by two aisles and chapels placed against the south wall belonging to Paduan families living in the parish (Forzatè, Fulgosio, da Rio and so on).

The church is entered through the portal in the façade in Lombard Renaissance style. On the north side, on the walls of the former Forzatè chapel, there is the *Crucifixion* and the *Birth of John the Baptist*, all that remains of a fresco cycle by Gerardino da Reggio which was executed c.1372.

A 14th century family sarcophagus in red Veronese marble is now in the first chapel on the south wall; in the latter there is an interesting triptych depicting the *Virgin and Child with Saints*, attributed to a follower of Giovanni Bellini of the late 15th century.

In the second chapel there is the *Holy Family and Saints* by Giandomenico Tiepolo (1777), completed by Giambattista Mengardi. In this chapel and the following one there is a series of four wooden bas-reliefs depicting scenes from the lives of saints attributed to Giovan Battista Viani, called Vianino (late 16th century).

MONTE DI PIETÀ (C3). Founded in Padua in 1491, in 1530 the Sacro Monte received a building situated in the Piazza del Duomo from the Venetian Republic; this was known as the *casa brusada* ("burnt house") and formerly belonged to the Carrara family. From 1531 to 1535 Giovanni Maria Falconetto restored and completed the arcades (attributed to Fra' Giovanni degli Eremitani) and added the upper floor to the building. In 1534 Domenico Campagnola was commissioned to execute the paintings of *Saint Bernardino da Feltre* in the arcade; these were restored in 1618 by Giovan Battista Bissoni, who added another painting of Bernardino over the third door. Gasparo Giona painted the *Almsgiving of Saint Bernardino* over the west arch of the arcade in 1618.

On the upper floor, now used for exhibitions, hangs the huge painting by Luca Ferrari depicting the *Virgin Saving Padua from the Plague* (1635), formerly in the now demolished church of Sant'Agostino.

Monte di Pietà, façade.

Arco Vallaresso, front. Padua was also struck by the plague in 1630 which was described in Alessandro Manzoni's I promessi sposi. *Among those who most distinguished themselves in succouring the population, which was decimated by the disease, was the Venetian capitano Alvise Vallaresso, to whom was dedicated the triumphal arch built next to the Monte di Pietà to give access to a courtyard in the former Carrara palace. Attributed to Giovan Battista della Scala, who is believed to have started building it in 1632, it combines typically Palladian features with an attempt to recreate an antique monument.*

The Religious Centre

It appears that the bishop's palace existed in the heart of the *insula* as early as the 4th or 5th centuries; in fact, it was sited next to the *umbilicus*, that is the point where the two main city streets, the *cardo* and the *decumanus*, crossed. In this area were also sited the cathedral, the baptistery and the cemetery situated on the site of the ancient pig market; this was given by Francesco Novello da Carrara to the bishop in 1401 (it is now the area in front of the cathedral). The unfinished façade in bare brick of the **Cathedral of Santa Maria** is placed on the east side. To the north of the cathedral is situated the **Baptistery of San Giovanni**. On the south side of the piazza, dominated by the square bulk of the **Sala dei Vescovi** flanked by small towers, stands the **Collegio Sacro**, attributed to Domenico Cerato (18th century); this replaced the old Scuola di San Sebastiano, in which there were frescoes by the circle of Mantegna (fragments in the Museo Civico). Next to it is Via Vandelli; the first turning on the right is Via Vescovado which ends at the **Roman bridge** of San Giovanni delle Navi, rebuilt in 1285. On the right stands the massive structure of the **Palazzo Vescovile (Bishop's Palace)** with its accumulation of styles from various periods.

Leaving the Bishop's Palace and going along Via Dietro Duomo behind the apses the route proceeds to Via dei Tadi, the old street leading to the bridge of the same name on the Vicenza road, which was rebuilt in 1300, as a column erected on the far end attests. On the other side of the bridge on the right is the Riviera San Benedetto: on this is the imposing **Palazzo dei Pisani de Lazara** (architect G. Selva, 1783, decoration by Pietro Antonio Novelli) and further on, set back from the road on the left, is **San Benedetto Vecchio**, one of the oldest churches in Padua. Going back along the Riviera to the right and crossing the iron bridge built in 1881, our route now passes through a gap in the remains of the medieval walls and takes us left into Via San Pietro, where the church of **San Pietro** is situated, formerly known as San Pietro *in palatio*.

Baptistery, Cathedral and Palazzo Vescovile (Bishop's Palace).

Opposite
Giusto de' Menabuoi, Annunciation, detail. Baptistery.

Giusto de' Menabuoi,
Virgin and Child. Cathedral,
Sacrestia dei Prebendati.

Nicoletto Semitecolo, Trinity.
Cathedral.

Opposite
Nicoletto Semitecolo, Scenes
from the Life of Saint
Sebastian. Cathedral,
Sacrestia dei Prebendati. In
the Sacrestia dei Canonici in
the cathedral there are seven
small panel paintings with
scenes from the lives of Saints
Sebastian, Marcus and
Marcellinus, painted by the
Venetian Nicoletto Semitecolo
in 1367: once placed back to
back, the paintings probably
formed the cover of a reliquary
on which were displayed, on
the outside, the lives of the
saints and inside pictures of
saints.

CATHEDRAL (C3). The first Paduan *domus ecclesiae* was probably built in the 4th c.; having been destroyed during the Lombard invasion of 602 A.D., it was rebuilt, only to be razed to the ground once again in the Hungarian invasion and yet again rebuilt: Bishop Ulrich consecrated it in 1075, but in 1117 the building was partially destroyed by an earthquake. After it had been rebuilt by the architect Macillo with a nave flanked by two aisles it was reconsecrated in 1180. It was only in 1547 that Bishop Francesco Pisani began the reconstruction on the basis of a project by Andrea da Valle (Sansovino and Michelangelo also provided drawings), under the direction of the chief architect Agostino Righetti from 1551 onwards. However, the work lasted right through the 17th c.; it was still unfinished in 1754 because the façade designed by Girolamo Frigimelica had not been built.

The interior consists of a nave flanked by two aisles covered with two domes, side chapels and two sacristies at the sides of the presbytery, which is built over the crypt and preceded by wide transepts. In the south aisle the **Chapel of San Gregorio Barbarigo** contains an altar by G. Massari (1762) with statues by F. Androsi; on the left-hand wall of the south transept there is the *Sarcophagus of Cardinal Pileo da Prata*, attributed to P. Dalle Masegne (before 1411); opposite is the *Monument to Pietro Barozzi*, attributed to A. Vittoria (c.1560). On the *Altar of the Blessed Sacrament* by G. Gloria and G. Massari there are statues by Tommaso Bonazza and J. Gabano, who also executed the bronze reliefs depicting *Scenes from the Gospels*. In the **Sacrestia dei Canonici** is a *Virgin and Child* by Giusto de' Menabuoi. In the presbytery there are large wooden choir stalls executed by Vicentine carvers to a design by F. Parodi (1693-94) and in the **Chapel of the Madonna dei Miracoli**, in the north transept, above the Baroque altar (Matteo Carneris, 1648) there is a *Virgin and Child* formerly attributed to Giotto, a copy of a painting by

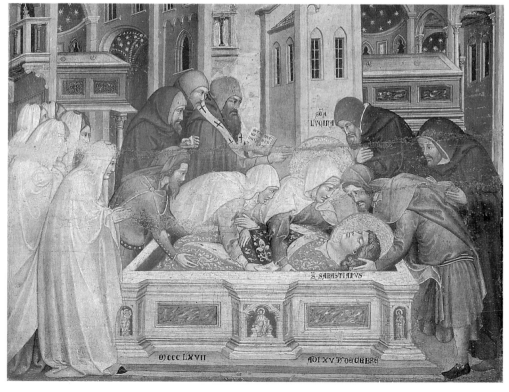

Baptistery, exterior.

*Giusto de' Menabuoi,
Polyptych. Baptistery.
The painting no longer has a
frame, which was destroyed as
the result of a recent theft.
Reassembled and replaced on
the altar, it depicts the Virgin
and Child enthroned,
surrounded by scenes from the
life of John the Baptist, titular
of the baptistery, saints and
doctors of the church.*

Giusto de' Menabuoi now in the Sacrestia dei Canonici. In the nave, by the fourth pillar on the south side, is a wooden pulpit with a carved relief by Filippo Parodi (1692) and by the main entrance stands a holy water stoup, an early work by A. Bonazza.

BAPTISTERY (C3). It was probably built at the end of 1200. In 1378 Fina de' Buzzaccarini, the wife of Francesco I da Carrara, Signore of Padua, laid down in her will that both she and her husband should be buried here. The Florentine artist Giusto de' Menabuoi was commissioned to execute the decorations in the interior, illustrating the building's twin function of baptistery and funeral chapel; he completed this task by 1378, the year of Fina's death. The story of the salvation of humankind starts from the dome with *Heaven* which revolves around the Byzantine Christ the Pantocrator.

In the drum of the dome are depicted, in 33 scenes, episodes from the Old Testament, from the *Creation of the World* to *Joseph sold into Slavery by his Brothers*, annotated with inscriptions drawn from Genesis. The *Evangelists* and *Prophets* on the pendentives between the Carrara coats of arms have the function of linking the episodes of the Old Testament with those of the New Testament, which are recounted on the four walls, starting with the *Annunciation to Zacharias* on the north wall and ending with the *Ascension of Christ* over the east door, including scenes from the life of Saint John the Baptist. The cycle of scenes from the salvation concludes in the small apsidiole, on the dome of which there is the *Pentecost* and, on the walls, 43 scenes from the *Apocalypse* based on the Revelation of Saint John the Divine.

Above the altar there is a *Polyptych* by Giusto de' Menabuoi.

PALAZZO VESCOVILE (BISHOP'S PALACE) (C3). It stands on the south side of the cathedral with its medley of various styles from different periods, beginning with the 14th c., when Bishop Pagano della Torre built the main body until the end of the 17th c., when the south wing was added. The 14th century main portal gives onto Via Dietro Duomo: in the architrave there are a pair of late *Roman busts* reused to represent Emperor Henry IV and Empress Bertha.

Inside there is the vast **Sala dei Visconti** (approx. 500 sq.m) which occupies the interior of the large structure visible from the Piazza del Duomo; its name derives from the frescoes with *Portraits of Paduan Bishops* (up to 1484) painted by Bartolomeo Montagna; in a niche there is a *portrait of Petrarch* (14th century), which was previously in the poet's house in Via Dietro Duomo. The hall gives access to the **Cappella Vescovile** (Bishop's Chapel), a small room decorated with frescoes by Jacopo da Montagnana (1494) depicting *Apostles and Evangelists*; he also painted the triptych of the *Annunciation* over the altar (1495). The floor in polychrome ceramic tiles made in Urbino with the coat of arms of Bishop Barozzi, who commissioned the chapel, is remarkable.

Palazzo Vescovile, Cappella Vescovile.

From the new wing of the bishop's palace there is access to the **Biblioteca Capitolare**; founded in the 12th c. and opened to the public in the 15th c. this is well endowed with codices and manuscripts, including *Isidore's Evangeliary*, decorated with splendid miniatures of 1170, and the *Epistolary of Giovanni da Gaibana* of 1259. The **Sala del Museo Diocesano** (Room of the Diocesan Museum) may also be reached; this was decorated by J. da Montagnana with a frieze in antique style and a *Resurrection* over the south door.

Palazzo Vescovile, Salone dei Vescovi.

Deposition, 13th century fresco. Church of San Benedetto.

Church of San Benedetto, façade.

CHURCH OF SAN BENEDETTO VECCHIO (B2). According to contemporary sources the monastery and church of San Benedetto were founded in 1195. Around 1259 the Benedictine nuns took over the monastery, where they remained until the dissolution in 1810, when the building became the parish church of San Leonardo. Restoration work was carried out from 1938 to 1944, but the church was seriously damaged by the bombing in that year which also destroyed the frescoes depicting *Scenes of the Apocalypse* by Giusto de' Menabuoi; by 1952 it had been rebuilt.

The interior, with both Romanesque and Gothic elements, consists of a nave covered with a timber-trussed roof and flanked by two aisles with cross-vaults. In a niche in the entrance wall in the nave there is a fresco depicting the *Deposition* by a late Duecento painter from Veneto; above the third altar in the south aisle there is the *Death of Saint Benedict* by Pietro Damini. The high altar dates from 1695; the statues on the reredos are by Tommaso Allio and are surrounded by complex architectural decorations by G.G. Veri (1663); the altarpiece depicting the *Transfiguration* is by A. Maganza.

On the sides of the presbytery there are two large paintings: the *Multiplication of Loaves and Fishes* by Francesco Minorello and *Moses Drawing Water from the Rock* by Alessandro Varotari, called Padovanino. In the chapel on the north side of the presbytery the altarpiece depicting *Christ with Saints* is by Domenico Tintoretto, while in the sacristy on the south side there are various paintings by Baroque artists.

CHURCH OF SAN PIETRO (C3). One of the oldest churches in Padua, it was mentioned in 9th century documents and was destroyed during the Hungarian invasions of the 10th century; it was rebuilt before 1026 and in that year was entrusted to the canonesses of San Pietro. Having been rebuilt, probably in the 14th century, it was restored in 1480, then in the late 16th century. The interior consists of a nave and two aisles of different sizes covered with cross vaults. Above the second altar of the nave there is a painting representing the *Conversion of Saint Paul* by Palma il Giovane (1604). In the apse above the eighteenth century wooden choir stalls, there is a painting on stone representing the *Delivery of the Keys to Saint Peter* which has been variously attributed to Dario Varotari and Domenico Campagnola.

In the south aisle there is a *Pietà* by a 15th century Paduan sculptor and, on the east wall, *Saint Peter with Saints Paul and Benedict and Praying Nuns*, a stone relief in triptych form made by Marco and Andrea da Firenze in 1424.

The **Chapel of the Madonna di Loreto** was built in 1765 on the model of the Santa Casa of Loreto: in the ambulatory there are stucco panels with *Gospel Scenes* by a sculptor from Veneto in the circle of Giovanni Maria Morlaiter.

In the sacristy, which is covered by a sail vault, there are 17th century paintings.

Church of San Pietro, façade.

Marco and Andrea da Firenze, Saints Peter, Paul and Benedict, stone relief. Church of San Pietro.

S. PAULUS AP.   S. PETRUS AP. SACRARIUM VIRGINUM COLLEGIUM INEUNTE SAEC. XI SUAM PENES AEDEM EXCIPIENS   S. BENEDICTUS AB.

The Administrative and Cultural Centre

Around Via VIII Febbraio, the principal street of the city, which has now become a pedestrian precinct between the Canton del Gallo and Piazza Garibaldi, is the area in which the administrative and cultural life of Padua is concentrated. The street, which is parallel to the course of the River Brenta, was built on the site of the port, which was probably also that of the forum and certainly that of the Roman markets: here was set up (where there is now the Piazzetta Garzeria) the woollen-mill, which was one of the main productive enterprises of the past; here the **University** building was later located opposite the now demolished church of San Martino (on its site the town hall now stands); lastly the **Caffè Pedrocchi**, a monument to the social life of the 19th century, was established here.

The **town hall** fronts onto Via VIII Febbraio with a section that was built in 1922-30 as a memorial to the fallen of the First World War (Romeo Moretti and Giovan Battista Scarpari); it encloses a courtyard overlooked by the 16th century façade of the Palazzo del Podestà. To the south of this is the **Banca Antoniana building**, designed by Gio Ponti (1966) and built on the area of the site — of archaeological importance due to discoveries from the Palaeolithic period — of the Palazzo del Gallo which gave its name to the crossroads (*canton* in local dialect), because there was formerly a tavern here with a sign depicting a cock (*gallo*).

Moreover, there was an ancient inn on whose sign there was an ox (Bò in dialect). This was located in the block opposite

Palazzo Municipale (town hall), the hanging courtyard with a well-curb.

Opposite

Pietro Damini, Exchange of the Insignia of Power between the Two Podestà Valier, detail. Palazzo Municipale, Sala della Giunta.

University building, façade.

the town hall that was surrounded by Via VIII Febbraio, Via Cesare Battisti, Via S. Francesco and Via Ponti Romani (the canal was filled in during the sixties) and gave its name to the university, when it was founded, so that it is still referred to as il *Bò*.

To the north of the town hall, with a colonnaded façade, is the Caffè Pedrocchi.

UNIVERSITY (C4). The University of Padua dates from 29 September 1222 when a group of professors and students from Bologna, who were joined by students from Vicenza, were offered refuge by Bishop Giordano and the podestà Rusca with permission to found a new university which assumed the form of a free association of students grouped in *nationes*: cismontane or Italians, ultramontane or foreigners. In 1399 the existence of two universities was authorized, the original one of the "jurists" and that of the "artists," which included medicine, philosophy and arts, each headed by a rector. Degrees were conferred by the bishop and the three colleges of doctors: the jurists, the "physicians and artists" and the theologians. The University of Padua became particularly important after it had been designated the only university in the republic by the Venetians and obtained a new charter from Pope Eugenius IV in 1439 which increased its privileges. It did not have a single building until 1493 when the jurists took over the premises of the inn displaying an ox on its sign, followed by the university of the artists in 1522. From 1552 to 1601 the building was reconstructed, taking on its present form; later other buildings were incorporated, while it was thoroughly renovated in 1938-42 by the architect Ettore Fagiuoli.

By linking the old part to the wing constructed on the canal and Via C. Battisti in 1922 (the architect was G. Fondelli) the university came to occupy the whole block. The old wing may be reached through the new courtyard: the two-tiered loggia—Doric on the ground floor and Ionic above—in the old courtyard, designed by Andrea Moroni, is richly decorated with the coats of arms of rectors and students which were placed here from 1542 to 1688. It is dominated by the bell tower (at midday the bells play the tune of a well-known student song); this was formerly the tower of a house belonging in 1289 to the Carrara. The two staircases which lead to the loggia are both decorated with coats of arms: at the bottom of the right-hand one is a statue of *Elena Cornaro Piscopia* by Bernardo Tabacco (1678), commemorating the first woman graduate. From the upper loggia there is access to the rooms where the degree examinations of the various faculties are held. On the left is that of the Faculty of Medicine; this still has the original ceiling of the pre-existent building; the frescoes on the walls are by Achille Funi (1942), the portraits are of famous physicians and professors.

The door, above which there is Gerolamo Acquapendente's coat of arms, leads to the **anatomical theatre**, which was built by Gerolamo Fabrizi Acquapendente in 1594 and is the first of its kind in the world.

It has an elliptical plan and conical cross-section; in the centre there is a dissecting table, from where the bodies were despatched through a trap-door to an underground room; they were then buried in the church of San Martino which stood just opposite. Next to this is the **Faculty of Engineering Hall**, while the **Halls of the Faculties of Arts and Philosophy, Law and Science** also give onto the loggia; they are decorated by modern artists (Gino Severini, Guido Saetti, Luigi Strazzabosco). The loggia also gives access to the old great hall, now called the **Sala dei Quaranta** because of the forty *Portraits of Illustrious Professors* painted here by Giacomo del Forno in 1942; the supposed *Chair of Galileo Galilei* is kept here. From this hall the present **Great Hall** is reached; this was once the School of the Jurists where Galileo gave his lectures because of the large number of students attending. It was rebuilt in 1854-56 and then in 1942 by Gio Ponti; the walls are decorated with students' coats of arms, while on the ceiling there is a painting representing *Wisdom and Discipline* by Giulio Carlini. Next follows the "**basilica**," so called because of the way it is divided into a "nave" flanked by two "aisles" by tall columns; it is decorated with frescoes by Pino Casarini (1940-42) depicting *Scenes from the History of the University* of 1848 and adorned with busts of famous academics including Galileo Galilei.

Then there is the **Sala del Collegio Accademico** in which is located the bookcase decorated with carvings by Michele

University building, old courtyard.

Bartens (1698-1704) which was made for the convent of Santa Giustina. This point marks the beginning of the new wing, built in 1938-43 when Carlo Anti was rector and decorated by various contemporary artists. In the **rector's study**, furnished by Gio Ponti, there are works by Filippo de Pisis (1941), Giacomo Manzù and Marcello Mascherini together with 16th century copies of antique vases, formerly in the Mantova Benavides collection.

From the gallery the visitor descends the **rectorate staircase**, which was designed by Gio Ponti, who also painted the frescoes on the walls; at the bottom of the stairs, in the **Entrance-hall of the Heroes** is located a sculpture of *Palinurus* by Arturo Martini.

CAFFÈ PEDROCCHI (C4). The Bergamasque coffee-house keeper Antonio Pedrocchi commissioned the engineer Giuseppe Bisacco to construct the building, and he started the work in 1816-18; it was completed by the architect Giuseppe Jappelli, who was assisted by the engineer Bartolomeo Franceschini, from 1826 onwards. The problem of the irregular shape of the site was resolved by a project which provided for three façades, each fronting onto one of the three streets surrounding the café. They were coordinated stylistically thanks to a plan which added a commodities exchange and a foyer to the actual café area. The ground floor was inaugurated on 9 June 1831, while the first floor, which became the premise of the Società del Casino Pedrocchi from 1856 onwards, was completed in time for the first conference of Italian scientists in 1842. In the meanwhile (1842) the Neo-Gothic section, known as the "Pedrocchino," had been added on the west side; this was also designed by Giuseppe Jappelli, while the sculptural decorations were by Antonio Gradenigo; here the pastry-shop, called the *offelleria*, was opened. In 1891 the

Opposite
University building, rectorate staircase.

Caffè Pedrocchi.

Above and opposite
*Caffè Pedrocchi, three of the
rooms on the first floor.*

building was donated to the municipality of Padua, which, until 1916 respected the wish of the former proprietors to keep the café open at night (this practice was the origin of the expression "café without doors"). In 1950 restoration work was carried out; this included the opening of the gallery, with the consequent elimination of the old *offelleria*, and the creation of three doors giving onto Via VIII Febbraio. The café is housed in the series of rooms located between the two lesser façades: their names derive from the predominant colour of the wallpaper and Jappelli himself was responsible for their furnishings. It is reached from the loggias: the east one consists of Doric columns between pillars, while in front of the north one giving onto the Piazzetta Pedrocchi there are a pair of stone lions sculpted by Giuseppe Petrelli. The other north-facing loggia, symmetrical with the preceding one, also having a pair of stone lions in front of it and decorated with stuccowork by Petrelli, forms the entrance-hall for the main staircase leading to the first floor. Entering by the south loggia, the visitor first reaches the **Sala Bianca** (White Room), on the walls of which are affixed plaques commemorating the incidents of 8 February 1848 during which university students confronted the Austrian soldiers, and an inscription referring to Stendhal's visit to Padua and the café in 1815.

Next there is the **Sala Rossa** (Red Room); this is divided into three parts by Ionic columns and decorated with stuccowork by Petrelli depicting Day and Night and with maps by Peghin in stereometric projection with inverted hemispheres. Then follows the **Sala Verde** (Green Room), once reserved for smokers. From this room there is access to the **Sala Gialla** (Yellow Room) or **Sala della Borsa** (Exchange Room); this was rebuilt by Angelo Pisani in 1950. The main staircase in the northwest loggia leads to the first floor of the building, formerly the premises of the Società del Casino Pedrocchi; now one of the city's museums, it is also used for the staging of cultural events. Through the **Saletta Etrusca**, used as the cloakroom and decorated with Etruscan vase motifs, the **Sala Greca** is reached; this has an octagonal plan and is embellished with Greek decorative designs, with a fresco by Giovanni Demin depicting *The Man of Plato* (1842). On the left there is access to the **Sala Rossini**; opposite is the **Saletta Rotonda** with oil paintings of *Views of Rome* executed by Ippolito Caffi (1841-42). The Saletta Rotonda serves to link the various rooms with the spiral staircase leading to Pedrocchi's apartment on the top floor. From the Saletta Rotonda a narrow corridor on the left leads to the **Sala Ercolana**, with paintings by Pietro Paoletti representing the story of *Diana the Huntress and Fisherwoman* (c.1842); the south door leads into the **Sala Rinascimentale** which gives onto the loggia facing the town hall; on the ceiling is an unfinished and partially repainted representation of the *Triumph of Civilization* by Vincenzo Gazzotto (1842). A corridor which is now closed linked the Sala Rinascimentale to the "armoury": decorated in Neo-Gothic style, this was formerly the reading room of the Circolo Casino Pedrocchi and is located in the "Pedrocchino" wing, which is now used as offices.

On the right of the Sala Greca there is direct access to the ballroom, the Sala Rossini, which is named after the famous Italian composer; the walls are decorated with a motif representing the Napoleonic bee in brass on marble, while allegorical female figures ("Zephyresses") bearing crowns illuminate, together with the large chandelier, the upper level of the room and fictive curtains made of stucco and papier mâché frame the orchestra platform on which there is an inscription with a dedication to Gioacchino Rossini.

From this large hall, situated at the heart of the building, it is possible to reach, to the west, the **Gabinetto Moresco** (Moorish Room), a small room decorated with mirrors on which there are painted birds, flowers and the figure of an Arab drawing aside the fictive curtain; to the north is the recently restored **Sala Egizia** (Egyptian Room), which is painted dark blue and decorated with Egyptian motifs in stucco and plaster, including a copy of a statue of the goddess Sekhmet, sphinxes, cinerary urns and so on, attributed to Antonio Gradenigo and Giuseppe Petrelli; the latter was responsible for the cast-iron railings on the balconies of the loggia on the north side of the Sala Rossini, linking it externally to the main staircase.

Opposite
Caffè Pedrocchi, Gabinetto Moresco.

Caffè Pedrocchi, Saletta Rotonda, detail of the Roman Forum by Ippolito Caffi.

The Religious Buildings outside the City Centre

The economic and social development of the city from the 12th century onwards inevitably affected its layout. The migration to the cities of the 13th century as a result of economic growth (the woollen-mill) and cultural evolution (the university) gave birth to the suburbs, but the mendicant orders also had their part to play in this process. Dominicans, Augustinian Hermits and Franciscan Friars Minor, as had the Albigensian Benedictines previously, settled on the edge of the old city, forming new urban centres which, by linking up with the insula (where the old city had developed) determined the city plan which was to be given its definitive form by the 16th century walls. While the building of monasteries by the Dominicans of Sant'Agostino and the Benedictines did not give rise to any notable amount of urban development, because they remained on the west bank of the river, the same could hardly be said of the construction to the south, in the suburb of Rudena, of the monastery of the Friars Minor of Saint Anthony and to the north in the suburb of Porciglia, of the monastery of the Augustinian Hermits and that of the Carmelites in the densely populated suburb of Porta Molino. So it was that during the 13th century the bridges and old city gates were renovated, while improvements were made to what had now become city streets. Later on this was also the case with the Franciscan Friars Minor, who in the present Via S. Francesco, with the monastery, hospital and the Scuola della Carità, built a second Franciscan community.

Via S. Francesco is situated at the end of Via VIII Febbraio, on the left.

Passing on the right the supposed tomb of Antenor, the visitor should continue down this charming street: on the left with a medieval tower is the **Palazzo Zabarella**, then the **Palazzo Papafava** (now housing the ENEL—National Electricity Board—offices) with a frescoed façade. On the right begins the arcade of the old hospital of San Francesco, incorporating the church of **San Francesco**. Opposite the church stands the **chapterhouse of Santa Maria della Carità**, with frescoes by Dario Varotari. Further down Via S. Francesco on the left is Via Ospedale where the **city hospital** is located.

From Via VIII Febbraio, passing the Caffè Pedrocchi in a northerly direction, after the Piazza Garibaldi—in the centre of this stands a Roman column surmounted by a statue of the *Madonna* by Giovanni Bonazza—the visitor reaches the **Roman arena**. On the right is the Piazza degli Eremitani where the **church of the Eremitani** stands. In the building, which once formed part of the monastery of the Eremitani and was partially reconstructed after the wartime bombing which severely damaged the nearby church, are housed a number of the sections of the **Padua City Museum** (Musei Civici); these are now being installed here after having been moved from the old building in the Piazza del Santo and are still awaiting a permanent home. Closely linked to this museum is the **Arena Chapel** (known in Italian as the **Cappella degli Scrovegni** or **Santa Maria dell'Annunziata**).

To the south of Via VIII Febbraio, after the Canton del Gal-

City Hospital, façade on Via Ospedale.

Opposite
Frescoes by Giusto de' Menabuoi. Baptistery, dome.

Church of San Gaetano, façade.

The botanical gardens of Padua are the oldest of their kind in Italy. Founded in 1545 by Professor Francesco Bonafede, they were laid out by Pietro da Noale and Daniele Barbaro (he engraved the regulations displayed at the entrance) with the assistance of the chief architect Andrea Moroni. Consisting of a circular area enclosed by a balustrade on a low wall, it is subdivided into four sections, each specializing in particular types of plants. One of the most famous plants is "Goethe's palm" (the German writer visited the gardens in 1786).

Cornaro Loggia and Odeum.

lo, is Via Roma, a picturesque arcaded street. On the right, flanked by an elegant arcade with red marble columns, is the church of **Santa Maria dei Servi**; proceeding along Via Roma, across the Ponte delle Torricelle and straight on down Via Umberto I, the visitor comes to the **Prato della Valle**. On the south side of the Prato stands the complex of the convent and Basilica of **Santa Giustina**; at the far end of Corso V. Emanuele II is located the church of **Santa Croce** together with the **Oratory of the Redentore**. From Via VIII Febbraio and Via S. Francesco, the quickest way to the Basilica of **Sant'Antonio**, popularly known as "Il Santo," is to turn right at the turreted Palazzo Zabarella and to take Via del Santo. Adjacent to the church stands the **Scuola del Santo**; this is flanked by the **Oratory of San Giorgio**. From the Piazza del Santo the **Loggia and Odeum Cornaro** are a short distance away along Via Cesarotti, while the **Botanical Gardens** are just down Via del Museo, which passes the old City Museum building. From Via VIII Febbraio, passing under the arch of the medieval **Porta Altinate** in the Piazza Garibaldi and taking Via Altinate, it is not far to the church of **San Gaetano**, one of the most interesting examples of Baroque architecture and decoration in Padua. Further along Via Altinate stands the church of **Santa Sofia**, one of the oldest in Padua, while on the left of its continuation, Via Belzoni, is the church of the **Madonna Immacolata**.

CHURCH OF SAN FRANCESCO (C4). Its construction in 1416 was linked to the building in 1414, on the orders of Baldo Bonaffari, vicar counsellor to Francesco da Carrara, of the hospital of San Francesco. In 1502 this first aisleless building, with the apse flanked by two chapels, was extended, probably by Lorenzo da Bologna, and the work was completed c.1520 with two aisles, the transept and the large chapel being added. In the north aisle, in the second chapel, there are frescoes depicting the *Life of the Virgin* by Girolamo Tessari del Santo, commissioned in 1523 by the Scuola della Carità and completed in 1526.

Next to the presbytery is a *Monument to Pietro Roccabonel-*

la begun in 1498 by Bartolomeo Bellano and finished by Andrea Briosco; on the entrance wall over the main door, hangs the *Ascension* by Paolo Veronese, completed by Pietro Damini in 1625 because the lower part had been stolen.

CHAPTERHOUSE OF SANTA MARIA DELLA CARITÀ

(C4). The original meeting place of the Confraternita della Carità was in the chapel of the Immacolata Concezione, decorated with frescoes by Girolamo del Santo, in the church of San Francesco. In 1419 it was moved to rooms in the recently constructed hospital, then thanks to a bequest of Sibilla da Cetto in 1421, it was established in the benefactress's house opposite the church.

This is still the chapterhouse today; the upper room is decorated with frescoes by Dario Varotari (1579-81) depicting the *Life of the Virgin*.

The chapterhouse was formerly reached by a covered outside staircase, which is now no longer in use.

The upper room has a coffered wooden ceiling with a cornice decorated with the coats of arms of the confraternity borne

Church of San Francesco, view of the courtyard and campanile.

Girolamo del Santo, Life of the Virgin, detail. Church of San Francesco, Chapel of the Madonna della Carità.

Andriolo de' Santi, one of the two Carrara tombs. Church of the Eremitani, next to the main entrance.

by gilded carved angels, attributed to B. Bellano. Starting from the south-east corner the frescoes represent the *Expulsion of Joachim from the Temple*, then continue with *Joachim among the Shepherds*, the *Meeting at the Golden Gate*, the *Birth of the Virgin* and the *Presentation of the Virgin*. On the west wall, next to the *Assumption of the Virgin* in the centre, are portrayed the two benefactors *Sibilla da Cetto and her husband Baldo Bonaffari*: on the left is a male figure seen from behind, a fragment of a previous fresco decoration (c.1450). The frescoes continue on north wall with the *Wooers bringing the Rods*, the *Marriage of the Virgin*, the *Annunciation*, the *Visitation* (the inscriptions dated 1672 refer to restoration work carried out then) and the *Death of Joseph*; on the east wall there is the *Death of the Virgin* and the *Assumption*. This cycle is the last example of the decoration of a confraternity in Padua.

CHURCH OF THE EREMITANI (B4). The present building dedicated to Saints Philip and James dates from 1276 when the Commune of Padua, as a result of the supplication of the preaching friars of Sant'Agostino, decided to rebuild the chapel on the site of the present choir. At the beginning of the 14th century this aisleless church was provided with a trilobate keel roof by Fra' Giovanni Eremitani using, so it is said, the wood that was left over from the roofing of the Palazzo della Ragione, also the work of Fra' Giovanni. The ceiling gives greater uniformity to the nave; three-quarters of the way along its structure changes to conform to the apsidal area consisting of three chapels.
On either side of the main entrance are the *Tombs of Ubertino and Jacopo da Carrara* by Andriolo de' Santi (1345-51), which were originally in the demolished church of Sant'Agostino. On the south side is the *Door of the Months*, thus named after the reliefs on the exterior executed by the Flo-

Church of the Eremitani, façade.

rentine sculptor Nicolò Baroncelli (1441); next are the side
chapels: in the **Cortellieri Chapel** there are fragments of
frescoes by Giusto de' Menabuoi of c.1370; the second chapel
contains fragments of frescoes by Guariento di Arpo of
c.1350, while the third chapel houses the *Mandeli Tomb*, attributed to the sculptor Andriolo de' Santi. Next to the presbytery stands the **Ovetari Chapel**. When making his will in
1443 Antonio Ovetari specified that his chapel in the church
of the Eremitani should be decorated with scenes from the
lives of Saints James and Christopher. On his death in 1448
his widow Imperatrice commissioned the Venetian artists
Giovanni d'Alemagna and Antonio Vivarini to paint the
scenes from the life of Saint Christopher and the ceiling with
the Evangelists, while the Paduans Nicolò Pizzolo and Andrea Mantegna were engaged to execute the scenes from the
life of Saint James, the Assumption and the Doctors of the
Church in the apse and the bas-relief altarpiece. Giovanni
d'Alemagna had died by 1451, the date when the first part of
the work was completed: Vivarini withdrew and was substituted by Ansuino da Forlì and Bono da Ferrara, while Pizzolo
was killed in a quarrel, so that Mantegna was the sole painter
of the work, which he had probably finished by 1455, leaving
only the last two scenes from the life of Saint Christopher to
be completed subsequently. The cycle was destroyed by a direct hit from a bomb on 11 March 1944: because they had pre-

*Andrea Mantegna, Life of
Saint Christopher (destroyed
in 1944), detail. Church of the
Eremitani, Ovetari Chapel.*

*Andrea Mantegna, Martyrdom
of Saint Christopher, detail.
Church of the Eremitani,
Ovetari Chapel.*

Bartolomeo Ammannati, Monument to Marco Mantova Benavides.

Funerary stele in the form of a cippus with two lion cubs crouching on the pediment, first half of the 1st century A.D. Musei Civici agli Eremitani.

Opposite

Girolamo Romanino, Virgin Enthroned with Saints (Santa Giustina Altarpiece). Musei Civici agli Eremitani.

viously been detached, the last two panels depicting the *Martyrdom of Saint Christopher* and the *Transport of the Saint's Body*, as well as the *Assumption* in the apse, were saved and were replaced after the war, together with the panels of the *Martyrdom of Saint James* and *Saint Christopher Converts the Knights*, which were reconstructed from fragments retrieved from the rubble.

The terracotta altarpiece by Nicolò Pizzolo depicting the *Virgin and Child Enthroned with Saints*, which shows the influence of Donatello's altar in the Basilica of Sant'Antonio, was also reconstructed from surviving fragments after the war. Besides the Ovetari Chapel, the Dotto Chapel and the presbytery decorated with frescoes depicting scenes from the lives of Saints Philip, Augustine and James the Less by Guariento di Arpo and Nicolò Semitecolo were also destroyed. The north wall has survived with scenes from the *Lives of Augustine and Philip*, allegorical figures of the *Planets* and human existence on the dado, as well as the large painted *Crucifix* (1370) by Nicolò Semitecolo. On the south wall is the *Coronation of the Virgin with Donors*, a fresco by Guariento di Arpo which formerly decorated the Carrara tombs in the church of Sant'Agostino. Next is the Sanguinacci Chapel, so called because it contains the tomb of this family, which is also decorated with frescoes: the *Virgin and Saints* is attributed to Giusto de' Menabuoi, while a 15th century terracotta sculpture on the altar represents the *Virgin and Child*. On the north wall is the *Monument to Marco Mantova Benavides*, executed from 1544 to 1546 by Bartolomeo Ammannati on the model of Michelangelo's Medicean tombs: *Time and Fame*, with *Immortality, Wisdom and Labour* flank the statue of the famous humanist and collector Marco Mantova.

PADUA CITY MUSEUM (Musei Civici) (B4). This is still being installed here after having been moved from the old building in the Piazza del Santo and is still awaiting a permanent home. On the ground floor, with displays designed by Franco Albini, is the **Museum of Archaeology**. This begins with the pre-Roman section, where artefacts found in the numerous necropolises in the area are exhibited (*Tomb of the Studded Vases*, 700 B.C.) and a unique series of Venetic stelae. A small room is dedicated to Etruscan, Italic and Venetic bronzes (6th-2nd centuries B.C.); after this there is the Roman section with a large number of portraits, monuments (*Bust of Silenus, Cippus of Toreuma, Aedicule of the Volumni*) and mosaics. A small room is devoted to the Paduan Egyptologist Giovan Battista Belzoni, with the two statues of the *Goddess Sekhmet*, formerly in the Palazzo della Ragione, which the explorer donated to the city of Padua; after other rooms with displays of Etruscan, Greek and Italiot artefacts there is the early Christian room in which the *Mosaic of Euterius* of the 4th century A.D. is exhibited. On the first floor is housed the **Museo Bottacin**; established in 1865 thanks to the bequest of Nicola Bottacin it contains over five thousand pieces, including coins, medals and seals (Roman medallions, Venetian series of coins, the *Mayr Cup*) and works of art, es-

Guariento di Arpo, Group of Twelve Seated Angels (Thrones). Musei Civici agli Eremitani.

Arena Chapel, façade. This photograph was taken in 1867.

Opposite

Arena Chapel, interior facing the entrance wall.

pecially 19th century (Gerolamo Induno, Lattanzio Querena, Vincenzo Vela): the Bottacin collection formerly included the panel paintings by Guariento representing the *Virgin and Child with Saints and Angels*, once on the ceiling of the chapel of the Carrara palace, now in the **Art Gallery**. This section, which begins with a *Crucifix* by Giotto, contains paintings from the 13th to the 16th centuries (Pietro and Giuliano da Rimini, Jacopo da Verona, Michele Giambono, Francesco Squarcione, Jacopo and Giovanni Bellini, Giorgione, Titian, Girolamo Romanino, Francesco Bassano the Younger, Palma Vecchio and Palma Giovane, etc.); at present it concludes with the Emo Capodilista collection, in which there are no less than 543 paintings, and the Renaissance bronze sculpture section (Andrea Briosco, Sansovino, Alessandro Vittoria, Francesco Segala, etc.).

ARENA CHAPEL (CAPPELLA DEGLI SCROVEGNI or SANTA MARIA DELL'ANNUNZIATA) (B4). On 6 February 1300 Enrico Scrovegni, a member of a rich family of bankers in Padua, bought the site of the city's Roman arena, where the house of the Delesmanini family stood. On 25 March 1303 the foundation stone of a new church dedicated to the Virgin of the Annunciation was laid on the orders of Enrico in order to atone for the sins of his father Reginaldo Scrovegni, a notorious usurer who was mentioned by Dante in the *Inferno* (XVII, 64-70). It was consecrated on 25 March 1305; later it was acquired by the Foscari from Venice together with the house, which was demolished in 1827, then it became

The fresco cycle in the chapel

Scenes from the lives of Joachim and Anna

1. Expulsion of Joachim from the Temple
2. Joachim's Return to the Sheepfold
3. Annunciation to Anna
4. Sacrifice of Joachim
5. Dream of Joachim
6. Meeting at the Golden Gate

Scenes from the life of the Virgin

7. Birth of the Virgin
8. Presentation of the Virgin at the Temple
9. Wooers Bringing the Rods
10. Wooers Praying for the Flowering of the Rods
11. Marriage of the Virgin
12. Bridal Procession of the Virgin
13. God the Father Sending the Angel Gabriel. The Annunciation

Scenes from the life and death of Christ

14. The Visitation
15. Birth of Christ
16. Adoration of the Magi
17. Presentation of Christ at the Temple
18. Flight into Egypt
19. Massacre of the Innocents
20. Teaching in the Temple
21. Baptism of Christ
22. Feast of Cana
23. Raising of Lazarus
24. Entry of Christ into Jerusalem
25. Cleansing of the Temple
26. Judas Receiving the Bribe
27. Last Supper
28. Washing of the Feet
29. Judas' Betrayal
30. Christ before Caiaphas
31. Mocking of Christ
32. Carrying of the Cross
33. Crucifixion
34. Lamentation
35. Resurrection and Noli me tangere
36. Ascension
37. Pentecost
38. Perspective of a chapel
39. Last Judgement

Virtues and Vices

a. Prudence
c. Fortitude
e. Temperance
g. Justice
i. Faith
m. Charity
o. Hope
p. Despair
n. Envy
l. Faithlessness
h. Injustice
f. Wrath
d. Inconstancy
b. Foolishness

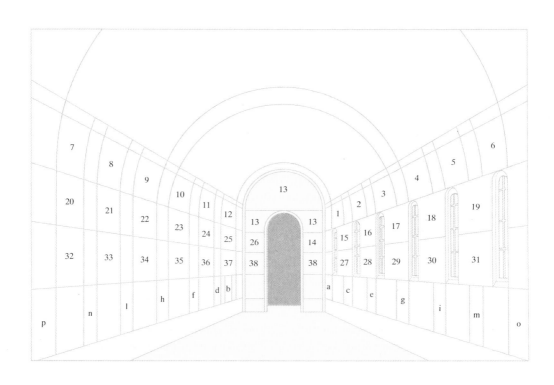

*Giotto, Meeting of Joachim
and Anna at the Golden Gate.
Arena Chapel.*

On the following page
*Giotto, Last Supper, detail.
Arena Chapel.*

the property of the Gradenigo Baglioni and finally it was pur-
chased by the municipality of Padua in 1880. The interior consists of an aisleless nave with a barrel vault and a small apse;
the latter was added subsequently to house the *Tomb of Enrico Scrovegni* (d. 1336), attributed to Andriolo de Santi. The
chapel is subdivided by a pair of altars which separate the area where the congregation assembled from that reserved for
the family.
The decoration of the interior was executed from 1303-05 by
Giotto, who had already worked for the Scrovegni in their
chapel in the Basilica of Sant'Antonio. The fresco cycle is
based on the concept of the salvation of mankind expressed
through the *Life of the Virgin and Christ*. The barrel vault,
painted deep blue and spangled with golden stars, is divided
by three bands—containing figures of kings and patriarchs
from the Old Testament—into two parts, in which preside
the *Virgin of Charity with Child and Prophets* in the area intended for the congregation and the Saviour and Four Prophets in that reserved for the Scrovegni family. On the wall of
the chancel arch, above the *Annunciation, Christ Enthroned
with Angels* is painted on a panel which functions as a balcony
for a small window. The episodes begin in the top register of
the south wall with scenes from the life of Joachim, then continue with those regarding Mary on the north wall; after the
Annunciation the life of Christ is related in spiral fashion,
first in the middle and then in the bottom registers, alternat-
ing between the south and north walls and concluding with
the *Pentecost* next to one of the two illusory views of a small
chapel on each side of the apse which appear to be a continuation of the nave. The high dado is painted with imitation
marble panels which frame fictive niches in which there are
allegorical images in grisaille of *Virtues* and *Vices*, both con-

cluding with the *Last Judgement* on the entrance wall, the
Virtues leading to Heaven and the Vices to Hell. The representation of the Last Judgement, devised as a huge painting
which two angels roll up at the top, centres on *Christ Enthroned in a Mandorla*, surrounded by angel choirs and
Apostles. On the right of Christ the blessed ascend to Heav-
en, while on his left the damned are dragged off by devils to
infernal torments. Below Christ the kneeling figure of Enrico
Scrovegni offers the chapel to the Virgin so that she might
present it to Christ. The decoration of the chapel was completed in the apse with the cycle of the *Death of the Virgin* by
Giotto's assistants and the *Virgin and Child with Angels* by
Giovanni Pisano on the high altar. In the sacristy the statue
portraying Enrico Scrovegni is thought to have been executed by a Venetian sculptor in 1320.

*Church of Santa Maria dei
Servi, with arcade.*

CHURCH OF SANTA MARIA DEI SERVI (C3). Work on
the church was begun in 1372 on the orders of Fina Buzzaccarini, the wife of Francesco il Vecchio da Carrara, and continued at least until 1392, when her son Francesco Novello assigned the church and the attached monastery to the order of
the Servites, thereby fulfilling the wishes of his father, who
had died in 1388. The interior, which is modelled on that of
the church of the Eremitani, consists of an aisleless nave with
a timber-trussed roof; there is a presbytery with a lancet
arch flanked by two small chapels with pointed arches. On
the west wall stands the imposing Baroque altar of the *Virgin
of the Sorrows* by Giovanni Bonazza (c. 1710-30); over the sacristy door is a bronze monument to Paolo de Castro (1492),
variously attributed to Andrea Briosco and Bartolomeo Bellano, while in the small chapel to the left of the high altar is a
wooden *Crucifix* of the 15th century.

PRATO DELLA VALLE (E3). Domenico Cerato was commissioned by the podestà Andrea Memmo to create this vast
open space in 1775. In Roman times this low-lying marshy ar-

Prato della Valle.

Statues in the Prato della Valle.

ea was the site of a theatre (the Zairo) which served as a source of building stone. Thanks to the Benedictines of Santa Giustina it was once again given a public role; here the main civic events were held, from pageants such as the "Castello d'Amore" (Castle of Love) to the "corsa dei Barberi" (a horse race), and the Santo fair, which had hitherto been held in the Piazza del Santo, and was moved here in 1608. It was with commercial objectives in mind that Andrea Memmo decided to recover the area by draining it with a small canal, lined with seats and statues of personages linked to the city of Padua; this in its turn surrounds the Isola Memmia, which is reached by four bridges flanked by statues of Doges, replaced with obelisks by the French troops after the fall of the Venetian Republic. With its stone vases the island was intended to be both a public garden and a market, for which a number of exedras were built. The statues, beginning with that of Antenor, commissioned by Andrea Memmo himself in 1775, were placed here by private citizens until 1838.

At present the Prato, as it is commonly known, is being replanted—the plane trees have been killed by a disease—and the statues are being restored.

Basilica of Santa Giustina.

MONASTERY AND BASILICA OF SANTA GIUSTINA

(E4). About the middle of the 4th century A.D. a basilica dedicated to the martyr Saint Justina of Padua was erected in the burial area outside the walls; it was rebuilt in the 5th century by Opilione, who added an oratory dedicated to Saint Prosdocimus where, from the 9th century onwards, there was a Benedictine community. After the monastery had been destroyed by an earthquake in 1117, the reconstruction was completed by 1124; it was enlarged in the 14th century by the addition of the **Chapel of Saint Luke**. The Renaissance period started with building of the new presbytery and sacristy, which was still in progress in 1476 and was continued at the end of the century with a project for a centrally planned building by Girolamo da Brescia. After the work had been interrupted due to the war with the League of Cambrai, in 1516 it was continued using a project by Andrea Briosco, called Riccio, then in 1520 the third project by Matteo da Valle was approved; he was then replaced by Andrea Moroni in 1532, who was chief architect until 1560. Thus the building was completed except for the façade and the roof; the former was left unfinished, while the latter, after Vincenzo Scamozzi had prepared a project that was never executed, was only completed in the 17th century when, inspired by Baldassare Longhena's designs, the altars in the aisles and the Cappella del Santissimo (1675) were built. The last Baroque addition was the Altar of the Pietà, executed by Filippo Parodi in 1698. The interior is on a Latin-cross plan with a nave flanked by two aisles and two orders of piers, covered with a barrel vault and eight domes, while the presbytery and choir are built over the crypt. On the entrance wall the painting of the *Presentation of the Podestà Cavalli* to Christ by Saint Mark is by Domenico Campagnola (1562). In the chapels in the two aisles there are sculptures and paintings by Baroque artists

Paolo Caliari called Veronese, the Martyrdom of Saint Justina, detail. Museo Civico.

such as Sebastiano Ricci, Antonio Zanchi, Luca Giordano, Valentin Lefevre, Giovanni Comino, Bernardo Falcone, M. de Surdis and so on. In the north transept is the *Tomb of Saint Luke* made by a sculptor from Veneto in 1313: in the apse there is a 16th century copy of the *Constantinopolitan Madonna* in a frame made by Amleto Sartori in 1960. On the altar in the next chapel there is a statue of *Blessed Arnaldo* by Bernardo Falcone (1681), flanked by Saint Peter and Saint Paul respectively attributed to Michele Fabris, called Ongaro, and Orazio Marinali (1682) and *Angels* by Heinrich Meyring; behind are remains of the 16th century altar by M. de Surdis. Next there is the **Cappella del Santissimo** with frescoes by Sebastiano Ricci (1700) representing *God the Father in Glory* in the apse and the *Adoration of the Holy Sacrament by the Apostles* in the vault.

On the altar by Giuseppe Sardi (1674) there is a tabernacle by Lorenzo Bedogni and Pier Paolo Corberelli (1656), while the antependium is decorated with intarsias by Antonio Corberelli; the bronze sculptures are by Carlo Trabucco (1679) and the other sculptures are by Alessandro Tremignon (1675). Giusto Le Court executed the two angels in 1675. In the presbytery, which was rebuilt in 1623, the high altar by Giovan Battista Nigetti is decorated with intarsias by Pier Paolo Corberelli (1640). At the side is a baldachin for the exhibition of the monstrance in carved walnut by Riccardo Taurigny, who also made the imposing wooden choir stalls (1558-66), which are carved and inlaid with scenes from the Old and New Testaments, and the lectern with the cupboard for the choir books in the middle with the *Life of Saint Justina* (1566-72). On the apse wall, in an elaborate frame carved by

Medieval sculptures formerly on the architrave of the portal of the Basilica of Santa Giustina.

Filippo Parodi, Altar of the Pietà. Basilica of Santa Giustina.

Giovanni Manetti (1576), is the *Martyrdom of Saint Justina* by Paolo Veronese (1575).

To the south of the presbytery is the **Chapel of the Pietà** decorated with stuccowork by Filippo Parodi, who also executed the marble group of the *Pietà* on the altar (1689). Next to this, on the wall of the **Chapel of Saint Maximus** is the *Jewish People in the Desert* by Francesco Maffei (c.1657); on the altar by Alessandro Tremignon (1680), incorporating the pre-existent 16th century one by M. de Surdis, is *Saint Maximus* by Michele Fabris, which was executed in 1681, as were the *Angels* by Heinrich Meyring, *Saint Philip* by Giovanni Comino and *Saint Bartholomew* by Bernardo Falcone. The door in the east wall of the Chapel of Saint Maximus leads into the **Corridoio delle Messe** (Corridor of the Masses), on the right of which is the **Chapel of Saint Luke**, formerly the chapterhouse (14th century), with frescoes of the *Life of Saint Luke* by Giovanni Storlato: in 1453-54 the *Saint Luke Polyptych* by Andrea Mantegna, now in the Brera Gallery, Milan was placed here. The corridoio delle messe leads to the **Large Corridor** (1538), where there are fragments of the old 12th century portal of the basilica; this gives onto the **Old Choir**, which was built in 1472 incorporating the medieval church, and consists of two bays and an apse. The carved and inlaid wooden choir stalls were executed by Francesco da Parma and Domenico da Piacenza (1467-77), who also made the cassone in the centre. To the south of the choir is the antechamber of the sacristy where the carved 12th century ar-

chitrave of the door of the Romanesque basilica is kept with *Scenes from the New Testament*; the lunette from this, depicting the *Church Offering the Eucharistic Wine*, is in a neighbouring room. Back in the church, in the middle of the south transept is the *Tomb of Saint Matthias* by Giovanni Francesco de Surdis (1562); behind this there is the entrance to the **Corridoio dei Martiri** (Corridor of the Martyrs) where there is a well decorated with niello work in which the bones of the martyrs were found (sculptures by followers of Francesco Segala and a small altarpiece by Pietro Damini).

Basilica of Santa Giustina, Chapel of Saint Prosdocimus.

From this corridor there is access to the **Chapel of Saint Prosdocimus** (1564), which incorporates the early Christian oratory built c.520 by the patrician Opilione (restored 1957). In the antechamber is the pediment with a dedicatory inscription (5th-6th century); in the chapel on the right the **Altar of Saint Prosdocimus** is made from a Roman sarcophagus found here in 1564; above this is a marble *Clypeate Image of Saint Prosdocimus* (5th or 6th century) preceded by a 5th century iconostasis.

CHURCH OF SANTA CROCE (F3). A church dedicated to the Holy Cross (Santa Croce) was recorded as early as 1181 near to the quay on the Canal of the Battaglia, which came from Este and Monselice. It became a parish church in 1308 and was restored from 1546 and 1563; in 1607 it was assigned to the Chierici Regolari Somaschi.

Rebuilding work was started in 1737 by the Somaschi friar Francesco Vecelli, who completed the work in 1745. The interior consists of an aisleless nave; on the ceiling there are frescoes depicting the *Triumph of the Cross* by Niccolò Baldissini, who also decorated the apse.

Over the main door is a *Guardian Angel* by Giovan Battista Mariotti, who also painted the altarpieces: on the left is *Saint Jerome Emiliani*, on the right *Saints Anthony, Francis of Paola and John Nepomucen*, while *Saint Helena Venerates the Cross* is in the presbytery.

BASILICA DI SANT'ANTONIO (D4). This is popularly referred to as **Il Santo**.

After Brother Anthony had died on 13 June 1231 his body was translated to the little church of Santa Maria Mater Domini, in the old-established suburb of Rudena, next to the monastery of the Franciscan Friars Minor. In 1232 Anthony was canonized and as early as 1238 the work on the building of the new church had begun; this proceeded under the rule of Ezzelino da Romano, but it was only in 1256 that it started in earnest. In 1263, in order to carry out work on the site of Santa Maria Mater Domini, the saint's body was translated to the nave. Then the ambulatory was completed around the choir, which had already been built, and probably about 1290 the work had been finished, apart from the roof. In 1301 a reference to a new church was recorded, and in 1310 there was another translation of the saint's body, perhaps to a chapel in the ambulatory, while the roof was constructed; this had certainly been finished by 1350, when the saint's body

Church of Santa Croce, façade.

was translated for the last time to the present tomb. Over the centuries other sections were added to the building and rebuilding work was carried out: in 1372 the Chapel of Saint Felix was built; in 1394 the collapse of a bell-tower led to the height of the ambulatory being increased; in 1447 the presbytery was rebuilt by Donatello with a new altar and 1456 work on the **Gattamelata Chapel** started. During the 16th century particular attention was paid to the sculptural decoration, especially in the **Cappella dell'Arca** where the main sculptors present at the time in the Venetian Republic worked (Tullio Lombardo, Jacopo Sansovino, Tiziano Minio); the rebuilding of the choir took place in 1648, while the Sanctuary of the Relics was built by Filippo Parodi 1690. As a result of the fire of 1749 extensive restoration work was carried out by Giovanni Gloria and Sante Benato, which did not, however, cause the appearance of the building to be modified.

The interior of the church, which is built on a Latin-cross plan, comprises a nave flanked by two aisles with a large ambulatory and chapels radiating from the apse, with eight domes forming the roof. In the south aisle, at the second pier,

Basilica of Sant'Antonio, with the monument to Gattamelata on the left.

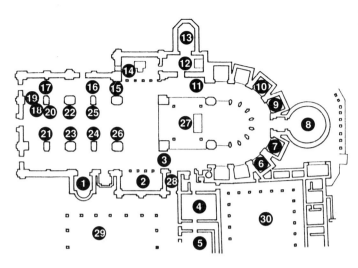

there is a painting of the *Martyrdom of Saint Agatha* by Giovan Battista Tiepolo (1736); opposite is the **Chapel of the Holy Sacrament**, built by Giovanni da Bolzano (1457-58) for Giacoma da Leonessa, the widow of Gattamelata (here was located the lost altarpiece by Jacopo, Gentile and Giovanni Bellini); it became the chapel of the Holy Sacrament in 1651 when it was rebuilt by Lorenzo Bedogni; it was again rebuilt by Lodovico Pogliaghi from 1927 to 1936, keeping the tombs of Erasmo da Narni and his son Giannantonio (Gregorio d'Allegretto, 1458). After this there is the **Santuliana Chapel** of 1624 next to the **Chapel of Saint Felix**, which was started in 1372 by Andriolo de Santi on behalf of Marquis Bonifacio Lupi di Soragna, the condottiere of the Carrara, and was completed in 1377. The sculptor executed the statues in the niches of the façade, while Altichiero assisted by Jacopo Avanzo painted the frescoes (1374-78) depicting the *Life of Saint James* taken from the *Golden Legend* by Jacopo da Varagine and the magnificent *Crucifixion* on the wall behind the altar. On the west wall is the *Presentation of Bonifacio Lupi and his wife Caterina to the Virgin* and, on the ceiling, *Prophets,* the *Symbols of the Evangelists* and the *Doctors of the Church.* The tomb of Bonifacio is to the right of the *Crucifixion.* Next there is a side door giving access along a passage—where there is the *Coronation of the Virgin* by Giusto de' Menabuoi—to the **Chapter Cloister**. After this, through a vestibule with a sail vault, the sacristy is reached; the ceiling of this is decorated with frescoes by Pietro Liberi (1665) depicting the *Glory of Saint Anthony.* On the right is a reliquary by Bartolomeo Bellano (1469-72), with intarsias by Lorenzo Canozi (1474-77); round the walls are cupboards decorated with paintings by Federico Suman (1847). Next to the sacristy is the **Chapterhouse** in which there are fragments of a fresco cycle attributed to Giotto and his workshop. Back in the church, on right the ambulatory begins, with the radial chapels decorated at the beginning of the 20th century by G.

Basilica of Sant'Antonio,
Cappella del Tesoro.

Cherubini, Ludovico Seitz and Biagio Biagetti. In the centre of the ambulatory is the **Cappella del Tesoro** (Chapel of the Treasure) built from 1689 to 1697 by Filippo Parodi, who executed the statue of *Saint Anthony in Glory* on the fastigium of the arch, the statues on the balustrade and the candleholders in the form of angels. Since 1745 the **Treasure of the Basilica** has been kept here: this consists of sacred vessels, relics and *ex voto* including the *Reliquary of the Saint's Tongue* by Giuliano da Firenze (1434-36) and the *Reliquary of the Cross* by Agostino Elini and Giovanni Fabbro (1437). Also displayed here are the two coffers of the saint's tomb and relics found during the examination of the body of Saint Anthony in 1981. The present choir, designed by Giorgio Massari, was constructed in 1753 as a replacement for the 15th century one made by Lorenzo Canozi (1462-69) after it had been destroyed by a fire in 1749, it had been installed here during the rebuilding of the presbytery by Lorenzo Bedogni in 1651. The whole of the apse is decorated with frescoes depicting the *Glorification of Saint Anthony*, begun in 1903 and continued for about forty years by Achille Casanova with the assistance of Edoardo Collamarini and Alfonso Rubbiani.
The presbytery was restored in 1895 by Camillo Boito, who placed the sculptures and bas-reliefs executed by Donatello in 1448 on the high altar: the *Virgin and Child* surrounded by *Saints Louis, Justina, Francis, Anthony, Daniel and Prosdocimus* and panels on the antependium with bronze bas-re-

liefs depicting the *Miracle of the Miser's Heart*, the *Miracle of the Irascible Son*, the *Symbols of the Evangelists* and behind the *Deposition* in stone, between the bronze reliefs of the *Miracle of the Believing Donkey* and the *Miracle of the Newborn Child*. Over the altar hangs the *Crucifix* (1443-44), next to it the *Easter Candelabrum* in bronze by Andrea Briosco (1507-15); on the pilasters of the apse, next to the presbytery are twelve bronze bas-reliefs depicting *Scenes from the Old Testament* by Bartolomeo Bellano (1484-88) and Andrea Briosco.

Altichiero Altichieri, Crucifixion, detail. Basilica of Sant'Antonio, Chapel of Saint Felix or Saint James.

In the north aisle is the **Chapel of the Madonna Mora**, part of the old church of Santa Maria Mater Domini, the name of which derives from the statue of the *Virgin Mary* attributed to Rinaldino di Francia (1396). On the north side of this chapel is the **Chapel of Blessed Luca Belludi**; consecrated in 1382, this was built by the Carrara administrators, the Conti family, who commissioned Giusto de' Menabuoi to paint the frescoes depicting *Scenes from the Lives of Saints Philip and James*. Next to the Chapel of the Madonna Nera is the **Chapel of Saint Anthony** where the *Saint's Tomb* is placed in the altar; designed by Andrea Briosco, it was built by Giovanni Minello from 1500 onwards and was completed in 1533 with the ceiling by Gian Maria Falconetto.

The altar was designed by Tiziano Aspetti (1593-94), who also executed the bronze statues, while Filippo Parodi (1689) and Orazio Marinali (1712) sculpted the groups of marble angels serving as bases for the candelabra at the sides. On the chap-

Donatello, Miracle of the Believing Donkey, detail. Basilica of Sant'Antonio, high altar.

el walls there are alto-relievos with the *Life of Saint Anthony* (Antonio Minello, Giovanni Rubino, Silvio Cosini, Danese Cattaneo, Girolamo Campagna, Jacopo Sansovino). In the first bay of the north aisle is the *Tomb of Antonio Roselli*, a professor of law at Padua university who died in 1466, by Pietro Lombardo (1464-67).

Opposite
Belludi Chapel with frescoes by Giusto de' Menabuoi. Basilica of Sant'Antonio.

On the first pier in the nave is the *Tomb of Alessandro Contarini*, the admiral of the Venetian fleet, designed by Michele Sammicheli (1553-58), with sculptures executed by various other artists: the *Slaves*, the *Nereid* and the *Fame* on the left are by Alessandro Vittoria, while the *Slaves* and the *Nereid* on the right are by Pietro Grazioli; the *Bust of Alessandro Contarini* is by Danese Cattaneo.

On the opposite pier, also by the artist Michele Sammicheli (1549), is the *Monument to Pietro Bembo* with a bust of the deceased by Danese Cattaneo and inscriptions furnished by Paolo Giovio.

The **Chapter Cloister** (c.1433) may be entered through the doorway to the right of the façade of the basilica; here there is a collection of tombs, gravestones and inscriptions of varied provenance. A passageway on the south side leads to the Cloister of the **Biblioteca del Generale**; here there is the entrance to the **Biblioteca Antoniana** where the original reliefs from Donatello's monument to Gattamelata are kept (*Putti Bearing Coats of Arms*) and the statue of *Saint Anthony* by Rinaldino di Francia (c.1392) which was formerly on the façade of the basilica.

In the hall of the Biblioteca Antoniana there are frescoes depicting the *Glory of the Virgin and Franciscan Saints* by Giovanni Antonio Pellegrini (1702) in a Rococo frame by Ferdinando Focchi and 18th century cupboards in briarwood; here are displayed two globes, celestial and terrestrial, by Father Vincenzo Coronelli, cosmographer of the Venetian Republic (early 18th century) and four showcases containing examples of codices, illuminated manuscripts and incunabula from the library's vast collection.

SCUOLA DEL SANTO (D4). Founded immediately after the death of Saint Anthony in 1231, the confraternity was provided with a meeting place in 1427.

An extra floor was added to this meeting place in 1504, while a staircase was built in the side wing in 1736 by Giovanni Gloria.

In 1510 the decoration of the upper room with frescoes was started; this has a coffered ceiling by Giovanni Cavalieri and Domenico Bottazzo (1506-10), while the dossals were executed by Girolamo da Piacenza. On the south wall, above the *Guardian Nicolò da Stra Distributing Bread to the Poor*, is the *Miracle of the Newborn Child* by Titian (1510-11), followed by the *Miracle of the Miser's Heart*, attributed to Girolamo del Santo (1511-12), who also painted the *Miracle of the Believing Donkey* (c.1514).

The cycle continues on the west wall with paintings by Filippo da Verona (1510), Girolamo del Santo (1513) and Bartolomeo Montagna (1512). On the right of the altar is the *Meet-

Scuola del Santo, façade.

Titian, Miracle of the Jealous Husband, detail. Scuola del Santo.

Oratory of San Giorgio, façade.

ing of Saint Anthony with Ezzelino by Giovanni Antonio Corona (1510-11); on its left is the *Preaching of Saint Anthony* (1509). On the east wall is the *Miracle of the Jealous Husband* (1511) followed by the *Miracle of the Irascible Son.* Then there are works by Girolamo del Santo (1524), Benedetto Montagna, Antonio Buttafoco (1755), Domenico Campagnola and Francesco Vecellio.

ORATORY OF SAN GIORGIO (D4). Originally the funerary chapel of the Lupi da Soragna family, it was built in 1377 by Raimondino Lupi, who commissioned Altichiero to paint the frescoes; these were completed by 1384. Formerly there was a tomb in the centre of the chapel; this was demolished in 1582, although a fragment of stone armour has survived. The fresco cycle depicts *Scenes from the Lives of the Saints George, Catherine and Lucy,* as well as *Scenes from the New Testament.* On the wall behind the altar is the *Coronation of the Virgin* and the *Crucifixion.* On the east wall is the *Life of Saint George;* opposite are *Scenes from the Lives of Saints Catherine and Lucy;* in the *Funeral of Saint Lucy* are portrayed personages of the Carrara court.

CORNARO LOGGIA AND ODEUM (D4). Having inherited a site near the Basilica of Sant'Antonio from his uncle, Alvise Angeleri, the writer of treatises and patron of the arts Alvise Cornaro commissioned Giovan Maria Falconetto to build a loggia to serve as a theatre; this was followed in 1530—the

architect was again Falconetto—by the *ottangolo* or odeum, the interior of which was decorated from 1533 to 1538. Thus was completed a complex which reflected the humanistic ideals of the cultural circle which gathered around Cornaro: Sperone Speroni, Pietro Bembo and Angelo Beolco, called Ruzzante. The loggia, with its echoes of the classical stage building, is comprised of five Doric arches in the lower tier, with architraves decorated with bucrania; over this is façade divided by Ionic pilasters and niches, surmounted by pediments, in which there are statues of *Diana*, the *Celestial Venus* and *Apollo* (attributed to Giovanni Rubino, called Dentone or Giovanni Mosca, called Zuan Padovano). In the lower loggia there is a tripartite vault which is decorated with frescoes by Giovan Maria Falconetto surrounded by frames embellished with stuccowork and a frieze; they depict *Perseus, Juno Punished by Jupiter* and *A Giant Struck by a Thunderbolt*. Next to the loggia the façade of the odeum is divided into two tiers: on the lower level, on either side of the central niche there are two aedicules containing the statues of the *Sun* and *Diana as Luna*; above there is a loggia with three arches in which there is a barrel vault.

On the ground floor, which is being restored, around a central octagon with niches there are rectangular rooms, based on the classicizing model derived from Giuliano da Sangallo. The fresco and stuccowork decoration clearly shows the influence of Roman and Mantuan classical models (grotesques, masks and mythological scenes) which are to be found at the

Cornaro Loggia, façade.

Cornaro Loggia, room in the odeum with stuccowork and frescoes.

Church of San Gaetano, frescoes in the dome.

Church of San Gaetano, interior.

Palazzo Te; it was executed by Tiziano Minio (1534-37) and Gualtiero Padovano with Roman and Mantuan assistants.

CHURCH OF SAN GAETANO (C4). The construction of this church began in 1582 thanks to the bequest of Bishop Alvise Corner; designed by Vincenzo Scamozzi and built under the direction of Bartolomeo Cavazza, it was finished in about 1586, when the building of the neighbouring monastery, also designed by Scamozzi, was started. Intended to house the Theatines, this was only completed in 1730.

The interior has an octagonal plan and is covered by a large dome with sixteen webs decorated with frescoes representing *Heaven* by Ludovico Vernansaal (c.1730); the stucco *Evangelists* in the pendentives are by a 16th century sculptor. The walls are covered with 18th century marble veneers and in the niches there are stucco sculptures by Ruggero Bascarpè (c.1585) portraying *Saints Peter, Paul, John the Baptist and Andrew.* In the first chapel on the south side there are paintings by Pietro Damini (*Saint Charles Borromeo Saves a Boy*) and Giovan Battista Bissoni (*Saint Charles Borromeo and Pope Clement VIII*); in the second chapel on the north side there is the *Presentation in the Temple* by Palma Giovane and the *Virgin and Child* attributed to Andrea Briosco. Behind the altar stands the large choir, decorated with *Theatine Saints* by Giovanni Battista Pellizzari and, on the end wall, the *Transfiguration* by an unknown Tuscan Mannerist. On the altar opposite the entrance there is the *Flagellation* by Ludovico Vernansaal and on the altar in the centre stands a wooden *Crucifix* by Agostino Vannini, a sculptor from Bassano. In the first chapel on the north side, dedicated to the cult of the crucifix, there are large numbers of 17th century paintings representing the passion of Christ hanging on the walls covered with marble veneers.

Church of Santa Sofia, façade.

CHURCH OF SANTA SOFIA (C5). This is one of the oldest churches in Padua: documents of 1123 state that here there was a sacred building constructed in 1106 which stood on the pre-existent foundations dating from the mid-9th century; it was built by Venetian workers, perhaps those who built the crypt of Saint Mark's.

The church consists of a nave with two aisles with an ambulatory: this is reflected in the façade, flanked by wings with sloping roofs, on a trachyte base.

In the austere interior the main decorative elements are the capitals and some fresco fragments, the oldest of which is a 13th century *Virgin and Child* in a niche located in the apse. The lunette in the apse was executed by followers of Giotto, while the *Pietà* on the second altar on the north side is by the sculptor Egidio da Weiner Neustadt (1430).

Church of Santa Sofia, interior.

CHURCH OF THE MADONNA IMMACOLATA (C5). The construction of this church took from 1853 to 1894; designed by Antonio Tosini, it was built on the site of the old church of Santa Maria Iconia. It has an aisleless nave, the upper part of which is decorated with frescoes depicting the *Life of the Virgin* by Giacomo Manzoni (19th century).

Works of art from the nearby church of Ognissanti were placed here. Next to the organ, on the entrance wall are paintings of *Saint John on Patmos* and the *Crucifixion* by Francesco Maffei; on the left wall is *Hagar and Ishmael* by Jacopo Marieschi. There is also a wooden *Virgin Mary* of the 15th century (Madonna dei Barcaioli) and the *Mocking of Job* by Gaspare Diziani. On the end wall there is the *Assumption of the Virgin* attributed to Sante Peranda and the *Virgin and Child* by Bonifacio de' Pitati and Jacopo Bassano (c.1543); in the presbytery there is *Heliodorus Driven from the Temple* and the *Slaying of Hagar* by Gaspare Diziani.

On the right wall of the nave is the *Miracle of Gideon* and *Joseph's Brothers Display his Bloody Coat* by Gaspare Diziani.

The City Walls

Little remains of the medieval city walls which, from 1195 until 1339, were constructed to defend the new suburbs as they were added to the city. The walls were built in three stages, corresponding to historical periods: the communal period (12th and 13th centuries), the period of Ezzelino and the communes (1237-1318) and that of the Carrara (c.1376). However, only two of the four main gates and fifteen minor ones have survived: the **Porta Altinate** on a Roman bridge with three arches (now buried) and the **Porta Molino**, at the end of a long Roman bridge with five arches that was rebuilt in 1830. The name of the latter derives from the many mills, floating or otherwise, which were formerly located here and were one of the factors contributing to the development of the area, where at an early date the friars of **Santa Maria del Carmine** settled and where there was already an important abbey, **San Giovanni da Verdara**. Together with the gates there is still the **castle**, built in 1242 by Ezzelino on the site of a pre-existent defensive tower called the Torlonga, and rebuilt from 1374 onwards by Francesco I da Carrara, who entrusted it to Nicolò della Berlanda; that it was at a strategically important point is demonstrated by the existence since ancient times of the church of **San Michele**, which was Byzantine or possibly Lombard.

After the siege of Padua in 1509 the Venetian Republic commissioned Bartolomeo d'Alviano and Sebastian da Lugano to replace the last walls built by the Carrara with ramparts, bastions and earthworks that extended for eleven kilometres round the city. At least half of these walls are still in good repair, and this is especially true of the gates: to the north-east stands the **Porta Ognissanti** or **Portello**, so called because of the ancient church of the same name situated in the vicinity (the small church of **San Massimo** is also close by) and the river port from which the *burchiello*, the boat linking Padua to Venice, departed; granted to the Bergamasque Guglielmo Grizi, it was built by M.A. Loredan in 1518. To the west is the **Porta Savonarola**, built in 1530 by Gian Maria Falconetto, who also constructed the **Porta San Giovanni** in 1528.

Porta Savonarola.

Opposite
View of the castle with the Torlonga (now an astronomical observatory).

Porta Molino.

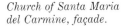

Lastly, to the east there is the **Porta Santa Croce**, erected next to the bastion of the same name which Michele Sanmicheli built around 1550, while the **Porta Liviana** or **Porta di Pontecorvo**—so called in honour of Bartolomeo d'Alviano, the commander of the Venetian army who supervised the building of the walls—are at present being restored.

CHURCH OF SANTA MARIA DEL CARMINE (B3). The friars of the Order of Our Lady of Mount Carmel settled in Padua near the Porta Molino at the end of the 13th century; it was only in the early 14th century that the building of a new monastery started, with an aisleless church which, however, collapsed in 1491. In 1495 Lorenzo da Bologna and Pietro Antonio degli Abati started the reconstruction on the basis of a project attributed to Father Bragazio; this was completed by Biagio Bigoio in 1523.

The aisleless nave, flanked by six chapels on each side, was covered by a vaulted roof with a large dome over the presbytery; the latter was destroyed by fire as a result of bombing in 1917 and rebuilt in 1931.

On the east side, towards the monastery, the sacristy was built in Renaissance style; Biagio Bigoio also built the chapter cloister (1513) with round arches. In the church itself, next to the entrance, on the stoups are statues of *Saint Albertus Magnus* and the *Virgin* by Giovanni Bonazza; on the

Church of Santa Maria del Carmine, façade.

entrance wall hangs the *Annunciation*, which formerly embellished the organ shutters, by Dario Varotari.

On the west wall, in the third chapel, is *Saint Mary-Magdalene of Pazzi* painted by Giulio Cirello (c.1671); in the **Chapel of the Holy Cross**, which follows, there are sculptures by Marc'Antonio de' Sordi on the altar by Bartolomeo Dindini (1562). Under the dome (decoration by Antonio Fasal, 1933-34) is the 18th century organ, the parapets of which are decorated with paintings of the *Life of Our Lady of Mount Carmel* by Giovan Battista Bissoni, which are linked to the translation in 1576 of the image of the *Virgin*, attributed to Stefano dell'Arzere, now standing on the high altar. Dating from c.1813, the latter was designed by Giovan Battista Salucci and Antonio Noale, with sculptures by Rinaldo Rinaldi (*Angels* bearing the statue of the Virgin).

On the east wall is the *Funerary Monument to Tiberio Deciano* (d.1582) with statues by Francesco Segala; in the **Chapel** formerly known as **Vigodarzere** is a painting of *Christ and the Mother of Zebedee's Sons* by Alessandro Varotari, called Padovanino.

The penultimate chapel, which houses the altar of the *fraglia dei mugnai* (the millers' guild), is decorated with marble inlays in Tuscan style.

Above the chapels on both side walls there is a cycle of paintings (mid-17th century), mainly by Paduan artists, depicting scenes related to the Carmelite order.

Church of Santa Maria del Carmine, cloister.

SCUOLA DEL CARMINE (B3). There had been a confraternity devoted to Our Lady of Mount Carmel in Padua since the beginning of the 14th century. In 1367 the new meeting place was built at the Carmelite monastery at the expense of Guglielmo Dal Sale; since it collapsed together with the church and the monastery in 1491, the following year it was housed in the friars' refectory, where it has remained until this day. Thanks to the Grompi and Cumani families, from 1505 to 1507 the interior was decorated with the *Scenes from the Lives of Joachim and Anna, the Virgin and Christ*. First of all the frieze with floral motifs was executed, then the Birth of the Virgin, the *Presentation of the Virgin*, the *Visit to the Temple* and the *Marriage of the Virgin*, attributed to Giulio Campagnola and assistants; he was replaced (c.1511-17) by Domenico Campagnola, who painted the *Meeting at the Golden Gate* and the *Adoration of the Shepherds*. After an interval the decoration was continued around 1530 by Girolamo del Santo, who painted the *Expulsion of Joachim from the Temple, Joachim among the Shepherds* and the *Life of Christ* on the south wall.

Around the middle of the 16th century a dividing wall was built to form an entrance hall: on this Stefano dell'Arzere painted the *Presentation of Christ at the Temple* and the *Adoration of the Magi*, as well as the *Nativity*, in which two donors are portrayed.

MONASTERY OF SAN GIOVANNI DI VERDARA (A3). The existence of this was first recorded in 1219, when it was a

Scuola del Carmine, façade.

On the following page
Frescoes by Domenico Campagnola and Stefano dell'Arzere. Scuola del Carmine.

Benedictine priorate. In 1436 it was taken over by the Lateran monks who in 1445 began the reconstruction of the complex by Lorenzo da Bologna and Giuliano da Porlezza.

It became an abbey in 1556, especially because of the importance of its role as a cultural centre; in 1783 it was suppressed together with the Congregation of the Laterans.

It then became an Austrian barracks; after 1852 it was used by the Jesuits and since 1866 it has housed the military hospital. Formerly the complex included a large church and three cloisters, of which only two have survived: the cloister with red Veronese marble columns, attributed to Pietro Antonio degli Abati (c.1492), and the large cloister with a two-tiered loggia and a well in the centre built by degli Abati and Lorenzo da Bologna in 1496. Next to them stands the church, consisting of a nave flanked by two aisles; it was begun around 1446 and is now part of the hospital.

On the upper floor of the building situated between the two cloisters, now used as a church, is the former **library** of the monastery; this is entered by a delicately carved portal in Lombard style. The hall of the library is covered by a barrel vault with lunettes, decorated with stone reliefs by Pietro Antonio degli Abati (1492).

On the north wall there are frescoes of the *Theological and Cardinal Virtues* and on the south wall the *Liberal Arts*, while in the blind windows there are *Portraits of University Professors* attributed to degli Abati.

Pietro Antonio degli Abati, A Professor in his Study. San Giovanni di Verdara (Military Hospital).

San Giovanni di Verdara, cloister.

Oratory of San Michele, façade.

Jacopo da Verona, Frescoes containing portraits of the Carrara, formerly in the Church of San Michele, now in the Musei Civici.
The present oratory, which is what remains of the ancient church of San Michele or Santi Arcangeli, perhaps of Byzantine origin, consists of the chapel dedicated to the Virgin which was built by Pietro de' Bovi (the Bovi were officials of the Carrara mint) in the church which was damaged in the conflict between the Carrara and Visconti armies around the nearby castle in 1390.
In 1397 Jacopo da Verona decorated the oratory with frescoes depicting the Life of the Virgin, the Evangelists and the Doctors of the Church; in them appear Francesco I and Francesco Novello da Carrara (Adoration of the Magi), together with members of the Bovi family.

ORATORY OF DI SAN MICHELE (D3). The present Oratory of San Michele, near the castle, was part of the church of San Michele or Santi Arcangeli, mentioned by the sources from 907 onwards, but probably dating from the 6th or 7th centuries. The chapel dedicated to the Virgin belonged to Pietro de' Bovi, who was in the employ of the Carrara family; he built it in 1397 (there is a tablet in the interior) after the fire in the church in 1390 which resulted from the conflict between the Carrara and Visconti armies. Jacopo da Verona decorated the interior and the entrance arch with the *Life of the Virgin, the Evangelists and the Doctors of the Church*. On the south wall there is the *Annunciation*, above the entrance arch, and a large fresco of *Saint Michael with Evangelists and Doctors of the Church* under the archway; on the east wall is the *Nativity* and the *Adoration of the Magi*. The frescoes on the north and west walls depicting the *Ascension, Pentecost* and the *Death of the Virgin* have been detached and are now in the City Museum at the Eremitani.

Selected Bibliography

C. Gasparotto, *S. Maria del Carmine di Padova*, Padua 1955.

Il Palazzo della Ragione di Padova, Venice 1963.

G. Beltrame, *Storia e arte in S. Tomaso Martire*, Padua 1966.

G. Brunetta, *Gli interventi dell'Università di Padova nel riutilizzo di antichi edifici*, Padua 1966.

L. Grossato, *Affreschi del Cinquecento in Padova*, Milan 1966.

J.K. Hyde, *Padua in the Age of Dante*, London 1966.

C. Semenzato, *La scultura veneta del Seicento e del Settecento*, Venice 1966.

A. Simioni, *Storia di Padova dalle origini alla fine del secolo XVIII*, Padua 1968.

S. Bettini, L. Puppi, *La chiesa degli Eremitani di Padova*, Vicenza 1970.

La basilica di Santa Giustina, Castelfranco Veneto 1970.

E. Rigoni, *L'arte rinascimentale in Padova*, Padua 1970.

G. Saggiori, *Padova nella storia delle sue strade*, Padova 1972.

Da Giotto al Mantegna, exhibition catalogue, Milan 1974.

Padova. Basiliche e chiese, edited by G. Bellinati and L. Puppi, Vicenza 1975.

Relazioni dei Rettori veneti in Terraferma. IV. Podestaria e Capitanato di Padova, Milan 1975.

Dopo Mantegna. Arte a Padova e nel territorio nei secoli XV e XVI, exhibition catalogue, Milan 1976.

A. Sartori, *Documenti per la storia dell'arte a Padova*, Vicenza 1976.

W. Wolters, *La scultura veneziana gotica 1300/1460*, Venice 1976.

G. Fabris, *Cronache e cronisti padovani*, Cittadella 1977.

Il Duomo di Padova e il suo Battistero, Trieste 1977.

Padova. Case e palazzi, edited by L. Puppi and F. Zuliani, Vicenza 1977.

A. Barzon, *Padova Cristiana*, Padua 1979.

C. Semenzato, *Il Palazzo del Bo. Arte e storia*, Trieste 1979.

G. Pavanello, "La decorazione neoclassica in Padova", in *Antologia di Belle Arti*, 1980, no. 13-14, pp. 55-73.

L. Puppi, *Il Caffè Pedrocchi di Padova*, Vicenza 1980.

L'edificio del Santo di Padova, edited by G. Lorenzoni, Vicenza 1981.

Padova antica. Da comunità paleovenata a città romana-cristiana, Trieste 1981.

La chiesa di Santa Sofia in Padua, Cittadella 1982.

L. Puppi, M. Universo, *Padova*, Rome and Bari 1982.

Giuseppe Jappelli e il suo tempo, acts of the conference, Padua 1983.

Il complesso di San Francesco Grande in Padova. Storia e arte, Padua 1983.

Le pitture del Santo di Padova, edited by C. Semenzato, Vicenza 1984.

Le sculture del Santo di Padova, edited by G. Lorenzoni, Vicenza 1984.

F. Cessi, *Padova medievale. Studi e documenti*, Padua 1985.

F. D'Arcais, "La pittura a Padova e nel territorio", in *La pittura in Italia. Il Duecento e Trecento*, edited by E. Castelnuovo, Milan 1986.

Prato della Valle. Due millenni di storia di un'avventura urbana, edited by L. Puppi, Padua 1986.

J. White, *Art and Architecture in Italy 1250-1400*, Harmondsworth 1987.

I Paleoveneti, exhibition catalogue, Padua 1988.

E. Saccomani, "La pittura a Padova e Vicenza nel Cinquecento", in *La pittura in Italia. Il Cinquecento*, edited by G. Briganti, Milan 1988.

P.L. Fantelli, "La pittura a Padova nel Seicento", in *La pittura in Italia. Il Seicento*, edited by M. Gregori and E. Schleier, Milan 1989.

A. Ventura, *Padova*, Bari 1989.

P.L. Fantelli, "La pittura dell'Ottocento a Padova e a Rovigo", in *La pittura in Italia. L'Ottocento*, edited by E. Castelnuovo, Milan 1990.

Photo Credits
Sergio Anelli, Milan
Electa Archives, Milan
Scala Archives, Florence
Drawings by Studio MARGIL

This volume has been printed
by Fantonigrafica – Elemond Editori Associati